Duvall — Best Wishes
and Good Luck —
always — Ali

SHAKESPEARE'S SELF-PORTRAIT

SHAKESPEARE'S SELF-PORTRAIT
PASSAGES FROM HIS WORK

❧ *CHOSEN, WITH NOTES, BY* ❧

A·L·ROWSE

A L Rowse

'In order to make a true estimate of the abilities and merit of a writer, it is always necessary to examine the genius of his age.'—Dr Johnson

UNIVERSITY
PRESS OF
AMERICA

Copyright © 1985 by

A. L. Rowse

First edition 1985
Reprinted 1985

University Press of America,™ Inc.

4720 Boston Way
Lanham, MD 20706

3 Henrietta Street
London WC2E 8LU England

Library of Congress Cataloging in Publication Data
Shakespeare, William, 1564–1616.
Shakespeare's self-portrait.
1. Shakespeare, William, 1564–1616—Quotations.
2. Shakespeare, William, 1564–1616—Biography.
I. Rowse, A. L. (Alfred Leslie), 1903–   . II. Title.
PR2771.R68   1985 C.2 822.3'3   84–15270
ISBN 0–8191–4220–4 (alk. paper)

Contents

ॐ

List of Plates

❧

1. William Shakespeare
   (Chandos portrait) The National Portrait Gallery
2a. Southampton at the time of the Sonnets
   (Hilliard miniature) The Fitzwilliam Museum, Cambridge
2b. Ralegh at the time of his fall
   (Hilliard miniature) The National Portrait Gallery
3. Elizabeth I at the time of the Kenilworth Entertainments
   (Hilliard miniature) The Courtauld Institute by permission of the
   Trustee of the Will of the 8th Earl of Berkeley, dec'd
4. King James I
   (Hilliard miniature) The British Museum
5. Essex in the 1590s
   The National Portrait Gallery
6. Lord Chamberlain Hunsdon, Patron of Shakespeare's Company
   The Courtauld Institute, by permission of the Trustee
   of the Will of the 8th Earl of Berkeley, dec'd
7. An Elizabethan Theatre
8. Holy Trinity Church, Stratford-upon-Avon, where Shakespeare
   was baptised and buried
   Allan Cash Ltd

To President Ronald Reagan
for his historic honour
to Shakespeare's profession

———

Shakespeare's Self-Portrait

All writers write out of their own personal experience and of their experience of the world they know. William Shakespeare is no exception to this rule, in fact he is the greatest example of it – and the most obvious, though few people are aware of it. Ben Jonson, who knew him well and found him irresistible, tells us, 'he was indeed honest [the Elizabethan word for honourable], and of an open and free nature'. That is to say that – though he was a very clever and subtle man – he was truthful and candid. He did not write any of his work to make a mystery of it. But he was writing four hundred years ago, so that one needs an intimate knowledge of the time he lived in to be able to interpret fully his many references to it and sometimes to catch the meaning and tone of his language, which became progressively more difficult, concentrated and elliptical.

Actually he is the most autobiographical of all Elizabethan dramatists, who reveals himself more fully and intimately in his works than any of them – as we should expect from 'an open and free nature'. In fact we know more about him than about any other Elizabethan dramatist, with the single exception of Ben Jonson's *later* career: we know far less about his early life than we do about Shakespeare, whose father the Alderman and his family were very well known in Stratford-upon-Avon.

William Shakespeare is the only one of the dramatists to have written his Autobiography, in the Sonnets, during the crucial and decisive years of his life, 1592 to 1594. Even here widespread confusion has been created, quite unnecessarily, by people not noticing the obvious fact that when they were published years later, in 1609, it was the publisher who dedicated them to Mr W.H. – not Shakespeare's young man at all, but the publisher's dedicatee. William Shakespeare wrote the Sonnets for the obvious person, his young lord and patron, Southampton, to whom he owed so much – and to whom he publicly dedicated his famous poems, *Venus and Adonis* and *The Rape of Lucrece* with his love and duty: 'the love I dedicate to your lordship is without end' – quite rightly, he owed so much to him. He had nothing whatever to do with the *publication* of the Sonnets: much too near the bone, too intimate and revealing of the private life of the three of them, the poet–actor–dramatist, his generous, rather spoiled young patron, and the remarkable character – now at last made plain to us – of the dark and equivocal young lady, Emilia Lanier *née* Bassano, musical and Italianate, discarded mistress of Lord Chamberlain Hunsdon, the patron of Shakespeare's Company.

My aim here is not to write Shakespeare's biography, but to let him write it for himself, in his own words, since no writer is more autobiographically revealing. In truth, he tells us everything about himself.

The rhythms of a man's speech are deeply personal, and correspond subtly – too subtly for abstract analysis – to the impulses of his heart's blood. And they are correspondingly recognisable, sometimes easily. Shakespeare's voice is most personal and recognisable. I remember hearing it one day unexpectedly, quoted in a slab of somebody's prose –

> Thou hast nor youth nor age,
> But, as it were, an after-dinner's sleep,
> Dreaming on both –

and suddenly found myself in tears. It was his personal voice coming to one across the ages.

He is no less recognisable in hundreds of lines:

> We, ignorant of ourselves,
> Beg often our own harms, which the wise powers
> Deny us for our good: so find we profit
> By losing of our prayers.

Or,

> Full oft 'tis seen,
> Our means secure us, and our mere defects
> Prove our commodities.

It is his unmistakable inflexion: it could only be he, and nobody else.

We border here on a great mystery in all modern art, which is inextricably linked with, expresses the personality of, the artist, composer or painter. (So that nothing could be more obtuse, or obscurantist, than the exclusion of the personal in some academic criticism.) How *is* it that we hear a phrase of Beethoven or Schubert, Chopin, Tchaikovsky or Debussy, and can recognise who is speaking? Or can at once recognise a Gauguin or Van Gogh, Seurat or Utrillo, a Rembrandt or Tiepolo or Bronzino – or a hundred others – in a few strokes of the brush? Or a Rodin, a Maillol, a Houdon – or an Eric Gill?

It is surely very mysterious, and at the same time rather wonderful. It applies no less, perhaps even more, to the greatest artists – Michelangelo, Bach, Shakespeare. With them we can even register the progression in style, with the development of the man's mind, from early to middle to late Beethoven, say, or similarly with Shakespeare.

The development of the style goes along with the thought that it expresses. So that it is again a mistake to suppose that we cannot recognise what Shakespeare thought. (Naturally, stupids cannot recognise anything.) But already, in those brief passages of only a few lines, we can detect characteristic thoughts of Shakespeare. Sometimes he makes it easy for us by repeating several times over a thought that evidently appealed to him.

It is often said conventionally that one cannot tell what a dramatist thinks because he puts both sides of a question. How imperceptive! – as if one cannot tell what Bernard Shaw thought, or any other dramatist for that matter: Brecht, Sartre or Montherlant, Marlowe or Ben Jonson. Shakespeare is no exception: he is a writer like any other, only subtler, more *ondoyant* like Montaigne. However, we know what Montaigne thought, and at one point Shakespeare flatly contradicts him – on the subject of primitive communism in *The Tempest.*

Moreover, it is superficial to object that, because both points of view are fairly put, there is no telling what a man thinks; for both points may be relevant and valid, and a man may well hold both in perspective, two sides of the diptych. We may take the two views of death in *Measure for Measure* – one as an extinction of the joys of life, the other as an end of our troubles: at one time the one view may prevail with a man, at another time the other. It does not prevent one from discerning a writer's values and choices, especially when – as a perceptive writer, Logan Pearsall Smith, diagnosed – one can hear the tone of voice. One can even hear it enforced in Shakespeare's repeated reflections on ingratitude, or on honour or reputation; on seeming and being, on what people really are and what they seem – an actor would be particularly conscious of that. When he writes,

'Tis not so above:
There is no shuffling, there the action lies
In his true nature, and we ourselves compelled
Even to the teeth and forehead of our faults
To give in evidence –

need we doubt that this is what he thought? It is utterly in keeping with what we know of him.

Or again, when he writes:

Why, all the souls that were were forfeit once;
And He that might the vantage best have took
Found out the remedy. How would you be
If He, which is the top of judgement, should
But judge you as you are?

Here we have the foundation of his Christian belief, again in keeping with expressions of it elsewhere.

And this is apart from his constant and continual enforcement of his obvious and positive views about society: the hatred of disorder, civil war, anarchy; the insistence upon the necessity of order and degree according to function; upon authority and obedience, a two-way relationship, for, if rulers fall down on their duty, their failure is brought home to them, as well as the fell consequences of the populace undermining social order. A humane man, who clearly hated cruelty, he saw that the breakdown of order led to even worse suffering than before. He saw how thin is the crust of civilisation, and – once broken up – what dark waters men are plunged into. Our own time has seen that dreadful lesson brought home to us on a wider scale than ever before. Since he had a deeper and more dependable knowledge of human nature than any other writer, he had no illusions. On a quite simple and positive plane, it is remarkable that he had a far more responsible understanding of politics and society than any of the Elizabethan dramatists.

Not the least remarkable thing about him – though no one has remarked it – is that he seems to have thought no nonsense at all, unlike Milton, at the opposite pole in our literature.

To come to the man, in the environment of his time, the approach of the historian of the age is indispensable. My own discoveries and findings –

in the firm dating of Sonnets and plays, thus providing the proper foundation for the chronological development of the work; the unanswerable solutions to the old vexed questions of the dedication of the Sonnets, to and for whom written; the identity of the Rival Poet and the Dark Lady, with the new light thrown on a number of the plays, in particular, *The Two Gentlemen of Verona*, *Love's Labour's Lost*, *A Midsummer Night's Dream*, *Romeo and Juliet* and *All's Well That Ends Well* – all this adds a dimension to our knowledge and will, given time, effect a revolution in Shakespeare studies, at present all too obviously scraping the barrel and much in need of a new impulse.

But revolutions have a conservative side to them, and all my findings, though definitive, are completely in accordance with tradition and all that we have hitherto known of him. Here I do not wish to interpose for long between the reader and Shakespeare himself: the whole point of this book is that the reader should see him in his own words. But it is necessary here to explain a few points.

Again and again I have noticed editors neglecting to explain references to contemporary persons and events, while going into endless irrelevant details about 'sources' from which Shakespeare did or did not derive his plots, excruciating bibliographical minutiae, the compositors who printed his work, their methods of punctuation, or lack of it, etc. Imagine the ineptitude, while neglecting the facts of the writer's personal experience and his reaction to what was going on around him at the time! Some editors, like E. K. Chambers or the editors of the New Oxford Shakespeare, obstinately refuse to recognise obvious contemporary references.

Everybody recognises the well-known references to Elizabeth I and James I, whom Shakespeare would have seen frequently enough, with their courtiers, from regular performances at Court. Everybody recognises the hopeful tribute in *Henry V* to Essex – Southampton's leader – on his leaving London for the Irish campaign in 1599. Then why not see that old Polonius in *Hamlet* is in part a caricature of old Burghley, as Dover Wilson realised? While Berowne in *Love's Labour's Lost* is a skit on himself, put in the mouth of his mistress, Rosaline, who herself is described in practically the same words as the Dark Lady in the Sonnets. Everybody knows that *Hamlet* has an extended reference to the rivalry of 1600–1 between the Boys' Companies and the Men's, the so-called War of the Theatres. Yet a recent edition of *Hamlet* goes out of its way to deny the obvious reference to the siege of Ostend of this very time, recognised again by Dover Wilson:

> I see
> The imminent death of twenty thousand men
> That, for a fantasy and trick of fame . . .
>   fight for a plot
> Whereon the numbers cannot try the cause,
> Which is not tomb enough and continent
> To hide the slain.

This is exactly as it was around Ostend in 1600–1, as an Elizabethan historian knows. To be able to decipher the contemporary references is a great help to the dating of the plays as of the Sonnets. And it is idiotic to throw away, or refuse to acknowledge, any information that can throw light on the life and work of our greatest writer.

Let us come to what he tells us about himself. A man's will sums up what he has arrived at in the course of his life, nothing better or more revealing. William Shakespeare's is that of a Stratford man, leaving property in and around his native town, who has made a modest fortune in the theatre in London. His success has confirmed the status he has won as 'gentleman', along with the best house in the town which it had enabled him to buy. His devotion to his native town is marked, and exceptional. Other theatre people – like Heming, Condell or Alleyn – put their winnings into property in or near London. Not so Shakespeare: he was bent on making a show in his home town, and recovering his father's losses (he did not succeed in getting back the property alienated to Uncle and Aunt Lambert out at Barton-on-the-Heath). He had recently bought half the gatehouse into the Blackfriars in London, a convenient *pied-à-terre*, and he leaves money for mourning rings to his three 'fellows', leaders along with him in the Company, Richard Burbage, its star, Heming and Condell. So – there we have the man: a Stratford townsman who has made good in the London theatre.

He is very much a family man. A good deal of his will is concerned with providing for his second daughter Judith and for various contingencies therewith. The bulk of the property was naturally to come to the elder daughter, the intelligent Susanna, and her doctor husband, John Hall. (He treated Shakespeare's fellow Warwickshireman, the poet Drayton.) Susanna, we know, ran the household; she and her husband would occupy the best double-bed. It was thoughtful of her father to allocate the next best bed for his widow; so – away with the rubbish written on that subject by people who do not qualify to write on it.

Shakespeare's only boy Hamnet – Hamlet is another form of the name, observe – had died in 1596, his name coming from his godparent, Hamnet Sadler, an old neighbour from early days in Henley Street. He received a bequest of money for a ring to remember him by. Shakespeare's residual heiress was Susanna's only child, little Elizabeth. For her second husband she was to marry a knight, Sir John Barnard – so she ended up a titled lady. She left the old home for her husband's country house; in her will she left money to her poor relations, the Hathaways, while her husband's consigned the lumber in the house at Stratford to be destroyed – no doubt papers and books among it, no-one left to be interested!

The will is a neighbourly one: the usual conventional bequest of a gentleman to the poor of the parish; the old home in Henley Street to his sister for life, with bequests of clothes – a valuable item in those days – and money to her and her three sons. His sword went to neighbour Thomas Combe, other bequests to several old friends; his godson, William Walker, was remembered with 20s in gold.

The invocation at the head of the will makes it clear that William Shakespeare was a conforming member of the Church: it recites the regular Protestant formula, where the Catholic formula invoking the Blessed Virgin and the saints is quite otherwise – and that disposes of the nonsense written on that subject. Everything shows that Shakespeare was a regular conforming Anglican, with an old-fashioned Catholic flavouring, though he read latterly in the Geneva Bible. One thing is quite clear: he was no Puritan.

A few family references are discernible in his work, in particular the touching lines expressing grief for his dead boy, written into *King John* in that year 1596. Nothing of the sort in Marlowe, for obvious reasons: he was a devoted, aggressive homosexual; nor is there any family feeling in Ben Jonson. Remarkably, there is far more about schooling and grammar-school education than in any other Elizabethan dramatist, or several of them together. Not only frequent tags from grammar school text books, but quotations from Latin texts used in school, notably the favourite Ovid. (He was himself to be hailed later as an English Ovid, i.e. essentially a poet of love.) Not only this, but we have specimens of school-teaching, how it was done, from the pedant Holofernes, and a regular Latin lesson for a young William in *The Merry Wives*. And schoolmasters are made regular fun of.

An early tradition, going right back to a member of the Globe Company, tells us that for a time Shakespeare was an usher at school in the country. His marked concern here is corroborated by the fact that his earliest plays are school plays. In an Elizabethan school comedy was represented by Plautus – grammar-school teaching was based on Latin; tragedy was represented by the stories from Ovid or Seneca. Well, the earliest comedy, *The Comedy of Errors*, comes out of Plautus; the earliest tragedy from Ovid, with Senecan horrors.

Shakespeare's schooling was, like Jonson's and Marlowe's, a grammar-school one, evidently at the local school, like theirs. It is clear that, though he did not go on to the university (no particular advantage to a playwright), he continued his education on his own. All real education is self-education; it oddly needs emphasising that he was a singularly clever man, read avidly and quickly, picking up tips from everybody, everywhere. When these things came together to bear fruit, they did so with an intense energy that gives the impression of having been dammed up, and the work burst upon the world with astonishing speed and success, which a senior in the field – and a university man to boot – Robert Greene bitterly resented. The actor turned dramatist proved well able to compete with the university men on their terms.

Before this turn came about there was a hiatus. The countryman was addicted to sport. A sonnet confesses his 'sportive blood', though this refers to his enthusiasm for women and sex. Sex had early trapped him into marriage with a woman considerably older than himself; a father at nineteen, by twenty-one he had a wife and three children to support. (*Very* unlike Marlowe, who could concentrate on his writing.)

Marlowe and Jonson were both urban types, by birth, rearing and career. Shakespeare was a countryman from first to last, and this shows all through his work. But also it shows how addicted he was to sport. His early work reveals a perfect obsession with deer-hunting, an easy familiarity with horse and hounds. Also we have hare-coursing, hawking, bowls – a rather gentlemanly game then – archery; we know where the butts were at Stratford, in the meads between the bridge and the present theatre. No time for sport in his later busy life – he must have devoted a good deal of time to it in those earlier youthful years.

However, he had a young family to support; his father's affairs – the Alderman and Bailiff (i.e. Mayor) neglected them for the town's business – had gone downhill; there was the family's standing to rehabilitate – after all, his mother was an Arden. He took to acting and the theatre; though the apprenticeship was harsh and distasteful – he tells us so, and how much, with his grand ideas, he resented it – he was on a moving escalator, it bore him upwards and eventually (after what a career!) home.

Anyone who cannot see that the author of his work, Sonnets as well as

Plays, was a man of the theatre ought – in Harry Truman's phrase – to have his head examined: sheer lunacy. There are scores of references to his profession, to the theatre and actors and acting – and from the inside point of view and experience of the professional, from the beginning to the end. What he has to say on these matters forms two of the bulkiest sections of this book.

No writer, not even Molière, was more a man of the theatre: not only an actor – and we are told that he was a good one – but dramatist and producer; a trustworthy business man, who sometimes received the cash for performances; a shareholder in the Lord Chamberlain's Company on its formation; eventually part-owner of the Blackfriars theatre.

No dramatic criticism in the age is so revealingly incisive as the instructions given to the touring actors in *Hamlet*. No need to go into detail here – read what he says. The whole emphasis is on naturalness in acting, as in life. This is what he stood for as against the prating and rampaging about the stage of earlier Elizabethan drama – *Tamburlane*, for example.

In that age it was thought more highly of to be a poet – poetry was never at a higher estimation in a society than in the Renaissance. To be an actor was distinctly lower in status, touring actors were apt to be classed as mere vagabonds. We find Shakespeare several times expressing bitter resentment at having to earn his living this way and his sensitiveness at his name being exposed to shame, even his nature receiving an impress as at a dyer's hand. He need not have feared. Several indications show that he had a grand idea of himself – Robert Greene's description of the genteel actor with the provincial accent and good conceit of himself corroborates this. Again, it is another indication of people's extraordinary (yet normal enough) imperception that they fail to notice the immense and challenging literary ambition that bore him up and accomplished such work. Observe closely what he writes in the section 'On Himself', while catching the tone of polite self-deprecation proper to a gentleman.

It is no less important to have an intimate knowledge of Elizabethan society for even an elementary understanding of his relations with his patron, young Southampton. He was an earl, a rising star in the firmament of Court and society, a devoted adherent of Essex. Shakespeare's insistence was always on being regarded as a gentleman – and his behaviour was in accordance: one of the few denizens of the stage to behave like one, nothing recorded against him. It was the fact of his gentility that enabled him to meet on terms of some equality with Southampton, expressing proper deference in the flowery language proper to a beautiful young peer (poets addressed the Queen as a deity), retaining always an inner independence while in fact depending on his patron for support, not only financial. One needs to be pretty subtle to catch the exact tone of this complex, not wholly unparalleled relationship – no wonder ordinary minds fail to do so and have made such a mess of it.

An American 'New Critic' described Shakespeare's feeling for the young patron as 'infatuation', and for his dark young mistress as something less. The truth is the precise opposite: Shakespeare was infatuated by the remarkable young woman, and makes it clear that his love for the ambivalent youth was not in the least sexual. The notorious Sonnet 20 states that firmly, categorically. When he dedicated *The Rape of Lucrece* to his patron in 1594 he affirmed publicly, 'the love I dedicate to your lordship is without end'. If that love had been of the sort that brought such notoriety and disapprobation to Marlowe, Oxford, Francis Bacon and his brother, it would not have been proclaimed to the world uncompromisingly like that.

Again one sees how several prominent novelists have been quite astray about that, though the fact is obvious enough. Everything shows from the whole of his work, and his life, that William was a normal heterosexual, though we might qualify – more than normally keen on women.

Here we must draw attention to a marked lacuna in this book, a great gap: Shakespeare's Bawdy. It is impossible to illustrate it, it is so omnipresent, on almost every other page. He is indeed one of the sexiest of writers. This element in him caused acute embarrassment to Victorian prudes, like Robert Bridges, but constitutes a preservative salty element of constant appeal to ordinary humans. There is actually much more of it than even these appreciate: the greater one's knowledge of Elizabethan language the more *double entendres*, innuendos, improper quips and hints one sees. They would not be lost on an Elizabethan audience, with appropriate gestures.

However, the psychological significance of this has been lost on modern imperceptives, even those who are not professors. Unthinkable as such a thought would be to an E. K. Chambers, bawdy talk is common enough with normal heterosexuals: it is uncommon with homosexuals like Marlowe or Francis Bacon, not characteristic, for obvious reasons. It is exceedingly characteristic of William Shakespeare; its omission here may be made good (or bad, according to taste) by consulting a whole book, by Eric Partridge, on the subject.

It is even necessary to repeat that people have been hopelessly confused by the dedication of the Sonnets, for want of familiarity with Elizabethan usage. (1) It was written by the publisher, Thomas Thorp, so that Mr W.H. was his man, not Shakespeare's young Lord. (2) 'Mr W.H.' could never refer to any lord whatever, but it was regular usage to refer to a knight as such; I have only recently learned that it was the rule in Tudor Parliaments to refer to knights as Mr (i.e. Master), plus surname, respectful but less pompous. (3) Southampton's young step-father, Sir William Harvey, was left the contents of the house when the old Countess died in 1607. He married a young wife in 1608; this is why Thorp is wishing him in 1609 all happiness and the eternity of having progeny – as Shakespeare had wished his young patron years before, if only he would do his duty and marry. 1607 – 1608 – 1609: all clear.

This Southampton would not do in those early years, and it is fairly clear that his seduction by the promiscuous Emilia Lanier was his first sexual experience with women. We know independently that he was homo-erotic, even after his belated and forced marriage in 1598. Shakespeare was responsible for this unfortunate introduction to the predatory Emilia – as the section from the Sonnets at this point shows; it added regret and anxiety to a complex situation, into which uncertainty, suspicion, jealousy (the Elizabethan word for suspicion) also entered.

Here too confusion has prevailed, quite unnecessarily. The poet Auden makes an elementary howler on the matter, writing that 'in Sonnet 20 Shakespeare speaks in frank, if not brutal, sexual terms of his friend's exclusive interest in women'! Completely wrong: a great deal is known about the young Earl, and he showed no interest in women until Emilia caught him. Evidently not much was known about Southampton by Auden, or much about the Elizabethan age either – or, for that matter, by a hopeless professor like Wilson Knight, who could see no Southampton at all, so plainly described in the Sonnets. Really, unless *drenched* in the Elizabethan age, poets, novelists, critics should not hold forth on what they do not, perhaps cannot, understand.

Since my discovery of who the Dark Lady was we can now appreciate what a remarkable personality hers was with whom the inflammable poet was infatuated. Shakespeare, in his open and free way, tells us everything about her except her name. But it was not until Thorp published the Sonnets years later, with their damning portrait of the young woman and the anguish she caused her lover, that she replied as a poet herself, with her own long religious poem, a flaming riposte inserted in prose against men for defaming women. She turned out a vehement feminist, unique for the age – a suitable candidate for Women's Lib.

One can sympathise with her: it must have become a bore to be pestered with the attentions of an impecunious actor years older than herself, when there were rich young earls of her own age about, however less inflammable. It is quite obvious, from Shakespeare's direct evidence, that she was not infatuated: her attitude to him was ambivalent. I am able to show something new here from the speaking evidence of *The Two Gentlemen* – inspired by the autobiographical conflict between friendship and love. His passion for her was not returned; in the situation he had to make way for the two young people; an element in what appeal the older man had for her was his 'wit', in both senses of the word – his intelligence and his jokes, 'a merrier man I never met withal'. An element in her appeal for him was her musicality – obvious enough, though we are given indications to that effect. He himself was the most musical, the most sensitively responsive to music, of all the dramatists.

I need say no more about these themes, so important in his life, Music and Love: let him speak for himself. Nor is there anything new to say about his relations with Christopher Marlowe, except that they were closer – for all the contrast in their natures and characters – than people have realised. Marlowe was ·an inspired genius, actually ahead of Shakespeare up to the time of his tragically early death; the junior of the two speaks of his senior with the deference – not untinged by regret – for his being one of the 'learned', and at length with a note of affection for the 'dead shepherd'.

Other contemporaries are clearly recognisable. I have brought together the references to the two monarchs from whom he and his Company received such marked favours. They performed twice as frequently at Court as any other Company – giving him a front-stage view, by the way, of the Court and Courtiers. Here he was on familiar ground wherever the Court happened to be, at Whitehall, Greenwich, Hampton Court, Windsor. *The Merry Wives* shows us how familiar he was with Windsor; nor need we doubt the ancient tradition that the Queen expressed a desire to see Falstaff in love, that the play was rapidly put together – it is mostly in prose, not that blank verse or rhyme gave him any difficulty – for a Garter Feast, for the play ends with a formal tribute to the Order.

Essex is another contemporary personality much to the fore, as indeed he was. Here there is something ambivalent, as in Essex's own personality. We can observe the movement of the observant dramatist's mind, from the hopeful tribute in *Henry V* of 1599, to the increasing dubiety as to his vertiginous behaviour, a favourite challenging the sovereign's power by which he rose, regret at his fall and followers deserting the fallen man, etc. Something of this is reflected in *Hamlet*, as Dover Wilson was historically sensitive enough to realise. Reflection upon it, the faction-fighting that led to it, disillusionment with the long war, are equally written into *Troilus and Cressida*, as an essential theme of the earlier experience with Southampton into *All's Well*.

It cannot be sufficiently emphasised that William Shakespeare was a conforming man; just because he saw through everything and everybody, he was not one to stick his neck out and get into trouble – unlike Marlowe and Jonson, or Nashe, Dekker, Middleton, or so many theatre folk. He was a gentleman – this is the meaning of the Elizabethan word 'gentle' constantly applied to him. The 'gentle Shakespeare' does not mean that he was soft in any sense (except perhaps in regard to women); it is obvious that his manners were courteous and polite, even rather grand – his language shows that – and qualified him for good society.

He was not a denizen of literary Bohemia, unlike Greene or Nashe, whose application for Southampton's patronage was not received. Shakespeare was really rather upstage, with a good opinion of himself, and completely identified himself with the governing class and its point of view. Nothing odd about that: it was merely common sense at the time – and not only for that time. He was a prudent, safe, normal man, a family man of good background – better than Marlowe's and Jonson's – on his way upward to becoming a man of property in his home town and county. One cannot but observe his superior, rather supercilious, attitude to the people: it is nearer to Swift's or Milton's than people appreciate, or perhaps – in these demotic days – like to think.

The people are always good for a joke: that is fair enough, with their malapropisms, their absurdities and misuse of language, their inconsistency and inability to keep a straight course in mind. Earlier, it is good-humoured enough, with positively affectionate transcripts from real life in such as Lance and his dog. We can hardly use the word affectionate of such dubious characters as Mistress Quickly, Mistress Overdone or Doll Tearsheet, but he certainly understood common humanity as well as he understood the burdens and follies of the great. The sympathy is for the individual human being. It is when we come to the collective entity, the People, the masses, the mob, that we see the contempt he had for them. Human foolery is at its maximum in the mass: no humbug about democracy with him. We need not go into it: let him speak for himself in the section devoted to the subject.

Similarly with tastes – so revealing of a man. A student of his imagery noticed the refinement of sensibility that marked his introduction into the aristocratic Southampton circle. This is what his nature really was, what it called out for in the years of resentment no less clearly expressed in the Sonnets. In these matters, most of all in his Reflections on life and its conduct, on manners and morals, religious belief – so sensitively and rarely touched on – we must let him speak for himself. In regard to contemporary events it is necessary that the historian should occasionally interpose with a note to explain what is being referred to, or to supply a significant bit of information.

In the section on Places that he knew, for example, *King Lear* has a description of what has come traditionally to be known as Shakespeare's Cliff. Well, the tradition receives some illumination at least from the fact that his Company was playing at Dover in August 1606; the play in which the description appears was first performed at Court on 26 December in the same year. The places round about Stratford that appear in *The Taming of the Shrew*, the forest of Arden of *As You Like It*, the Cotswold shearing-feast of *The Winter's Tale*, Justice Shallow's Gloucestershire orchard, all have the endearing interest that they were places familiar to Shakespeare from boyhood. And Warwickshire gets a good write-up in the earliest plays, *Henry VI*, as again in *Henry IV*.

The most sensitive register of the age was far more responsive to topical events than critics have realised, though Dr Johnson sensed it. We all know that *The Tempest* was sparked off by the wreck of the *Sea Venture*, driven in upon the coast of Bermuda – 'the enchanted isle' – on her voyage to Virginia in 1609. The account of the tornado and their experience on the isle, from the secretary to Virginia, came back to Blackfriars, where it came to Shakespeare's hand. He evidently read Hakluyt and the voyagers – influences noticeable in all the later plays. *Timon of Athens* picks up the craze for gold-digging of the Virginia colonists. *Macbeth*, with its tribute to the new Stuart dynasty, reflects the Gunpowder Plot of 1605. The theme of the Hundred Years War with France had a popular return to the stage with the Normandy campaign of 1591 – and Southampton crossed Channel to join in it. The Lopez affair of 1594 led to the revival of Marlowe's *The Jew of Malta*, which suggested *The Merchant of Venice* with its Italian–Jewish theme – and Emilia Bassano's family may well have been Italian Jews, as Southampton's tutor, Florio, was. Nor should one doubt the only proper dating of the reference in Sonnet 107 to 'the mortal moon' – the Queen frequently referred to as such. The *two* references in those lines coincide on one point: the emergence of the Queen from the shadow of danger from

Lopez, her doctor, charged with intending to poison her; and the peace promising olives of age in the surrender of Paris to Henri IV: i.e. early summer 1594, and the Sonnet is in correct chronological order.

The more one knows about these things the more they come together and corroborate each other. The life of the greatest writer in the language has been for too long the victim of conjectures, hence reduced to confusion – 'what a mess they have made of it', in Harold Macmillan's summary phrase – when what we need are the facts and the knowledge to interpret them.

For the rest let Shakespeare speak for himself and paint his own Self-Portrait.

Family

Does he not wear a great round beard like a glover's paring knife?
> *The Merry Wives of Windsor*, I.4.

... no bigger than an agate stone
On the forefinger of an alderman.
> *Romeo and Juliet*, I.4.

[Shakespeare's father, a glover, became an alderman.]

I could have crept into any alderman's thumb-ring.
> *1 Henry IV*, II.4.

Like rich hangings in a homely house.
> *2 Henry VI*, V.3

[Wilmcote, the home of Shakespeare's mother, Mary Arden, had eleven painted cloths hanging in various rooms – no ordinary farmhouse. This could well be a reminiscence, for the play is perhaps earliest of all.]

I loved the maid I married; never man
Sighed truer breath. But that I see thee here ...
           more dances my rapt heart
Than when I first my wedded mistress saw
Bestride my threshold.
> *Coriolanus*, IV.5.

[This play seems to have been written at home at Stratford in 1608.]

16

O, let me clip [embrace] ye
In arms as sound as when I wooed, in heart
As merry as when our nuptial day was done,
And tapers burned to bedward.

Coriolanus, 1.6.

Let still [ever] the woman take
An elder to herself: so wears she to him;
So sways she level in her husband's heart . . .
Our fancies are more giddy and unfirm,
More longing, wavering, sooner lost and worn
Than women's are . . .
Then let thy love be younger than thyself,
Or thy affection cannot hold the bent.

Twelfth Night, II.4.

[How revealing a comment this is! Young William at eighteen-and-a-half had married his Anne, a woman eight-and-a-half years his senior – a much greater age-gap then than now. Ten years later he was passionately engaged with Emilia, five-and-a-half years younger. We can hear the silence from Stratford.]

Looking on the lines
Of my boy's face, I thought I did recoil
Twenty-three years, and saw myself unbreeched
In my green velvet coat, my dagger muzzled
Lest it should bite its master, and so prove,
As ornaments oft do, too dangerous.

The Winter's Tale, 1.2.

Grief fills the room up of my absent child,
Lies in his bed, walks up and down with me,
Puts on his pretty looks, repeats his words,
Remembers me of all his gracious parts,
Stuffs out his vacant garments with his form . . .
I have heard you say
That we shall see and know our friends in heaven:
If that be true, I shall see my boy again.

King John, III.4.

[The play was finished, after revision, in 1596. Hamnet, Shakespeare's only boy, was buried, aged eleven, at Stratford, 11 August 1596.]

> when my old wife lived, upon
> This day she was both pantler, butler, cook;
> Both dame and servant; welcomed all, served all;
> Would sing her song and dance her turn; now here
> At upper end of the table, now in the middle;
> On his shoulder and his; her face o'fire
> With labour and the thing she took to quench it,
> She would to each one sip.

The Winter's Tale, IV.3

[From a late play, written 1610–11.]

School and Schooldays

Like a school broke up, each hurries towards his home.

2 Henry IV, iv.2

The whining schoolboy with his satchel
And shining morning face, creeping like snail
Unwillingly to school.

As You Like It, ii.7.

to sigh like a schoolboy that had lost his ABC.

The Two Gentlemen of Verona, ii.1.

Love goes toward love, as schoolboys from their books;
But love from love, toward school with heavy looks.

Romeo and Juliet, ii.2.

Evans, a Welsh schoolmaster: William, how many numbers is in nouns?
William: Two.
Evans: What is *fair*, William?
William: Pulcher.
Evans: What is *lapis*, William?
William: A *stone.*
Evans: And what is a *stone*, William?
William: A pebble.
Evans: No, it is *lapis*. I pray you remember in your prain.
William: Lapis.
Evans: That is a good William. What is he, William, that does lend articles?
William: Articles are borrowed of the pronoun, and be thus declined: *Singulariter, nominativo, hic, haec, hoc.*

Evans: Nominativo, *hig, hag, hog.* Pray you, mark, *genitivo, hujus.* Well, what is your accusative case?
William: Hinc.
Evans: I pray you have your remembrance, child: *accusativo, hung, hang, hog.* What is the focative case, William?
William: O *vocativo,* O.
Evans: Remember, William: focative is *caret* . . . What is your genitive case, plural, William?
William: Genitive case?
Evans: Ay.
William: Genitive, *horum, harum, horum.*

The Merry Wives of Windsor, iv.1.

Nathaniel, a curate: Very reverend sport, truly.
Holofernes, a schoolmaster: The deer was, as you know, *sanguis,* in blood; ripe as a pomewater, who now hangeth like a jewel in the ear of *caelo,* the sky, the welkin, the heaven; and anon falleth like a crab on the face of *terra,* the soil, the land, the earth.
Nathaniel: Truly, Master Holofernes, the epithets are sweetly varied, like a scholar at the least; but, sir, I assure ye, it was a buck of the first head.
Holofernes: Sir Nathaniel, *haud credo* [I hardly think so].
Dull, a constable: 'Twas not a *haud credo* [auld grey doe]; 'twas a pricket.
Holofernes: Most barbarous intimation! yet a kind of insinuation, as it were, *in via,* in way, of explication; *facere,* as it were, a replication; or rather, *ostentare,* to show, as it were, his inclination – after his undressed, unpolished, uneducated, unpruned, untrained or, rather, unlettered or, ratherest, unconfirmed fashion: to insert again my *haud credo* for a deer.
Dull: I said the deer was not a *haud credo:* 'twas a pricket.
Holofernes: Twice-sod, simplicity, *bis coctus!* O thou monster, Ignorance, how deformed dost thou look!
Nathaniel: Sir, he hath not fed of the dainties that are bred of a book; he hath not eat paper, as it were; he hath not drunk ink; his intellect is not replenished; he is only an animal, only sensible in the duller parts.

Love's Labour's Lost, iv.2

Like a pedant that keeps a school in the church

Twelfth Night, iii.2.

[It was usual for the curate to give elementary instruction to the young children in church.]

> *Integer vitae, scelerisque purus,*
> *Non eget Mauri jaculis, nec arcu.*
> O, it is a verse in Horace: I know it well:
> I read it in the grammar long ago.
>
> *Titus Andronicus*, IV.2.

> *Fauste, precor gelida quando pecus omne sub umbra Ruminat*, and so forth.
> Ah, good old Mantuan . . .
> Old Mantuan! Who understandeth thee not, loves thee not.
>
> *Love's Labour's Lost*, IV.2.

[A tag from school-use, typically the beginning of the first Eclogue.]

> Lucius, what book is that she tosseth so?
> – Grandsire, 'tis Ovid's Metamorphoses.
>
> *Titus Andronicus*, IV.1.

> Bargulus, the strong Illyrian pirate.
>
> *2 Henry VI*, IV.1.

[From Cicero's *Offices*, much used in school.]

> *Pene gelidus timor occupat artus.*
>
> *2 Henry VI*, IV.1.

[Shakespeare's memory has conflated words from Virgil with others from Lucan, much more familiar to Marlowe. It is noticeable that these tags, almost certainly from copy-book selections, occur in the early plays, when grammar-schooldays were not far away.]

> In my schooldays, when I had lost one shaft,
> I shot his fellow of the self-same flight
> The self-same way with more advisèd watch,
> To find the other forth. And by adventuring both,
> I oft found both.
>
> *The Merchant of Venice*, I.1.

> As willingly as e'er I came from school.
>
> *The Taming of the Shrew*, III.2.

> Never will I trust to speeches penned,
> Nor to the motion of a schoolboy's tongue.
>
> *Love's Labour's Lost*, V.2.

Sport

[It is observable how thickly these sporting references, especially to deer-hunting, fall in the early work of this out-of-doors countryman.]

What, hast thou not full often struck a doe
And borne her cleanly by the keeper's nose?

Titus Andronicus, ii.1.

Huntsman, I charge thee, tender well my hounds:
Brach Merriman, the poor cur is embossed,
And couple Clowder with the deep-mouthed brach.
Saw'st thou not, boy, how Silver made it good
At the hedge corner, in the coldest fault.
I would not lose the dog for twenty pound.
– Why, Bellman, is as good as he . . .
He cried upon it at the merest loss,
And twice today picked out the dullest scent:
Trust me, I take him for the better dog.
– Thou art a fool: if Echo were as fleet,
I would esteem him worth a dozen such.
But sup them well, and look unto them all –
Tomorrow I intend to hunt again.

The Taming of the Shrew, i.1.

[Brach means a bitch hound. Fault means a loss of scent. Embossed – foaming at the mouth.]

The hunt is up, the morn is bright and grey,
The fields are fragrant, and the woods are green.

22

Uncouple here and let us make a bay . . .
And rouse the prince and ring a hunter's peal.

Titus Andronicus, II.2.

We hunt not, we, with horse nor hound,
But hope to pluck a dainty doe to ground.

Titus Andronicus, II.2.

The preyful Princess pierced and pricked
       a pretty pleasing pricket;
Some say a sore, but not a sore
       till now made sore with shooting;
The dogs did yell; put 'L' to sore,
       then sorel jumps from thicket;
Or pricket, sore, or else sorel,
       the people fall to hooting.

Love's Labour's Lost, IV.2.

[A 'pricket' is a buck of the second year, a 'sore' of the fourth, and a 'sorel'
of the third – how well Shakespeare knew his deer! Bawdy implications
too – for those who understand them.]

Under this thick-grown brake we'll shroud ourselves,
For through this laund [glade] anon the deer will come.
And in this covert will we make our stand,
Culling the principal of all the deer.
– I'll stay above the hill, so both may shoot.
That cannot be: the noise of thy cross-bow
Will scare the herd, and so my shoot is lost.

3 Henry VI, III.1.

This way lies the game:
See where the huntsmen stand.
– Stand you thus close to steal the Bishop's deer?
Your horse stands ready at the park corner.

3 Henry VI, IV.5.

My love shall hear the music of my hounds,
Uncouple in the western valley; let them go;
Dispatch, I say, and find the forester . . .
My hounds are bred out of the Spartan kind,

So flewed [jowled] so sanded [sandy]; and their heads are hung
With ears that sweep away the morning dew;
Crook-knee'd and dew-lapped like Thessalian bulls;
Slow in pursuit, but matched in mouth like bells,
Each under each. A cry more tuneable
Was never holla'd to, nor cheered with horn.

A Midsummer Night's Dream, iv.1.

As the poor frighted deer that stands at gaze
Wildly determining which way to fly.

The Rape of Lucrece

Upon the brook that brawls along this wood . . .
                a poor sequestered stag
That from the hunters' aim had ta'en a hurt
Did come to languish . . .
The wretched animal heaved forth such groans
That their discharge did stretch his leathern coat
Almost to bursting, and the big round tears
Coursed one another down his innocent nose
In piteous chase.

As You Like It, ii.1.

A hound that runs counter, and yet draws dry-foot well.

The Comedy of Errors, iv.2.

Twenty crowns!
I'll venture so much of my hawk or hound.

The Taming of the Shrew, v.2.

He will spend his mouth, and promise, like Brabbler the hound.

Troilus and Cressida, v.1.

    when the fox hath once got in his nose,
He'll soon find means to make the body follow.

3 Henry VI, iv.7.

              coward dogs
Most spend their mouths when what they seem to threaten
Runs far before them.

Henry V, ii.4.

I do follow here in the chase, not like a hound that hunts, but one
that fills up the cry.

Othello, ii.3.

When night-dogs run, all sorts of deer are chased.

The Merry Wives of Windsor, v.5.

He is now at a cold scent.
Sowter will cry upon it for all this, though it be as rank as a fox.

Twelfth Night, ii.4.

But if thou needs wilt hunt, be ruled by me:
Uncouple at the timorous flying hare,
Or at the fox which lives by subtlety,
Or at the roe which no encounter dare:
Pursue these fearful creatures o'er the downs,
And on thy well-breathed horse keep with thy hounds.

And when thou hast on foot the purblind hare,
Mark the poor wretch, to overshoot his troubles
How he outruns the winds, and with what care
He cranks and crosses with a thousand doubles:
The many musits[1] through the which he goes
Are like a labyrinth to amaze his foes.

Sometime he runs among a flock of sheep,
To make the cunning hounds mistake their smell,
And sometime where earth-delving conies keep,
To stop the loud pursuers in their yell,
And sometime sorteth with a herd of deer:
Danger deviseth shifts; wit waits on fear.

For there his smell with others being mingled,
The hot scent-snuffing hounds are driven to doubt,
Ceasing their clamorous cry till they have singled
With much ado the cold fault cleanly out.
Then do they spend their mouths: Echo replies,
As if another chase were in the skies.

By this, poor Wat, far off upon a hill,
Stands on his hinder legs with listening ear,

---

[1] Hare's forms or lairs.

To hearken if his foes pursue him still:
Anon their loud alarums he doth hear;
And now his grief may be comparèd well
To one sore sick that hears the passing bell.

Then shalt thou see the dew-bedabbled wretch
Turn, and return, indenting with the way;
Each envious briar his weary legs doth scratch,
Each shadow makes him stop, each murmur stay:
For misery is trodden on by many,
And being low never relieved by any.

Venus and Adonis

    Let us score their backs,
And snatch 'em up, as we take hares, behind:
'Tis sport to maul a runner.

Antony and Cleopatra, iv.7.

Dost thou love hawking? thou hast hawks will soar
Above the morning lark. Or wilt thou hunt?
Thy hounds shall make the welkin [sky] answer them,
And fetch shrill echoes from the hollow earth.
– Say thou wilt course:[1] thy greyhounds are as swift
As breathèd stags, aye, fleeter than the roe.

The Taming of the Shrew, Induction, 2.

My falcon now is sharp and passing empty,
And till she stoop she must not be full-gorged,
For then she never looks upon her lure.
Another way I have to man my haggard,
To make her come and know her keeper's call –
That is, to watch her as we watch those kites,
That bate and beat, and will not be obedient.

The Taming of the Shrew, iv.1.

Believe me, lords, for flying at the brook,[2]
I saw not better sport these seven years' day:
Yet by your leave the wind was very high,
And, ten to one, old Joan had not gone out.

---

[1] Hare-coursing.
[2] i.e. at river birds, duck, etc.

– But what a point, my lord, your falcon made,
And what a pitch she flew above the rest!

2 Henry VI, II.1.

As wild geese that the creeping fowler eye,
Or russet-pated choughs, many in sort,
Rising and cawing at the gun's report,
Sever themselves, and madly sweep the sky.

A Midsummer Night's Dream, III.2.

As confident as is a falcon's flight
Against a bird.

Richard II, I.3.

When the wind is southerly I know a hawk from a handshaw [young heron].

Hamlet, II.2.

A falcon, towering in her pride of place,
Was by a mousing owl hawked at and killed.

Macbeth, II.4.

     like the haggard [wild hawk], check at every feather
That comes before his eye.

Twelfth Night, III.1.

     If I do prove her haggard,
Though that her jesses [strings] were my dear heart-strings,
I'd whistle her off, and let her down the wind
To prey at fortune.

Othello, III.3.

Between two hawks, which flies the higher pitch;
Between two dogs, which hath the deeper mouth . . .

1 Henry VI, II.4.

     O for a falconer's voice
To lure this tassel-gentle back again!

Romeo and Juliet, II.2.

We'll go a-birding together: I have a fine hawk for the bush.

The Merry Wives of Windsor, III.3.

> I bless the time
> When my good falcon made her flight across
> Her father's ground.
>
> The Winter's Tale, iv.3.

Slender: Why do your dogs bark so? Be there bears in the town?
Anne: I think there are, sir; I heard them talked of.
Slender: I love the sport well . . . You are afraid if you see the bear
loose, are you not?
Anne: Aye, indeed, sir.
Slender: That's meat and drink to me, now. I have seen Sackerson[1]
loose twenty times, and have taken him by the chain. But I warrant
you, the women have so cried and shrieked at it that it passed. But
women indeed cannot abide 'em; they are very ill-favoured rough
things.

The Merry Wives of Windsor, i.1.

Foolish curs that run winking into the mouth of a Russian bear, and
have their heads crushed like rotten apples.

Henry V, iii.7.

> They have tied me to a stake: I cannot fly,
> But bear-like I must fight the course.
>
> Macbeth, v.6.

> Are these thy bears? We'll bait thy bears to death,
> And manacle the bear-ward in their chains,
> If thou dar'st bring them to the baiting-place.
> – Oft have I seen a hot, o'er-weening cur,
> Run back and bite, because he was withheld;
> Who, being suffered with the bear's fell paw,
> Hath clapped his tail between his legs, and cried.
>
> 2 Henry VI, v.1.

Despite the bear-ward that protects the bear.

Ibid.

I will even take sixpence in earnest of the bear-ward.

Much Ado About Nothing, ii.1.

---

[1] A famous bear of the time.

A bear-herd, and now by profession a tinker.
The Taming of the Shrew, Induction, 2.

Like to an unlicked bear-whelp
That carries no impression of the dam.
3 Henry VI, iii.2.

He brought me out of favour with my lady about a bear-baiting.
Twelfth Night, ii.5.

He haunts wakes, fairs and bear-baitings.
The Winter's Tale, iv.3.

Enter bear.
Antigonus: I am gone for ever. [*Exit, pursued by bear.*]
The Winter's Tale, iii.3.

[This comic touch has been regarded as casual and improbable. Nothing improbable about it: it must have been frequent enough in Elizabethan streets.]

We'll play at bowls . . .
'Twill make me think the world is full of rubs,
And that my fortune runs against the bias.
Richard II, iii.4.

thus the bowl should run,
And not unluckily against the bias.
The Taming of the Shrew, iv.5.

Sometimes,
Like to a bowl upon a subtle ground
I have tumbled past the throw.
Coriolanus, v.2.

Was there ever man had such luck – when I kissed the jack, upon an upcast to be hit away! I had a hundred pound on't . . . What I have lost today at bowls I'll win tonight of him.
Cymbeline, ii.1.

Now let me see your archery:
Look ye draw home enough, and 'tis there straight.
Titus Andronicus, iv.3.

Lo, when a painter would surpass the life
In limning out a well-proportioned steed,
His art with nature's workmanship at strife,
As if the dead the living should exceed:
So did this horse excel a common one,
In shape, in courage, colour, pace and bone.

Round-hoofed, short-jointed, fetlocks shag and long,
Broad breast, full eye, small head, and nostril wide;
High crest, short ears, straight legs and passing strong,
Thin mane, thick tail, broad buttock, tender hide.

Venus and Adonis

His horse hipped with an old mothy saddle and stirrups of no
kindred; besides possessed with the glanders and like to mourn in
the chine; troubled with the lampass, infected with the fashions; full
of wind-galls, sped with spavins; rayed with the yellows, past cure of
the fives; stark spoiled with the staggers, begnawn with the bots;
swayed in the back, and shoulder-shotten; near-legged before, and
with a half-cheeked bit, and a head stall of sheep's leather, which
being restrained to keep him from stumbling, hath been often burst
and now repaired with knots; one girth six times pieced, and a
woman's crupper of velure . . . here and there pieced with pack-
thread.

The Taming of the Shrew, iii.2.

[This piece of comic virtuosity bespeaks his familiarity with horseflesh;
for the meanings of the terms, *v.* my edition to come in the *The
Contemporary Shakespeare.*]

On Himself

ẽ

Yet writers say, as in the sweetest bud
The eating canker dwells, so eating love
Inhabits in the finest wits of all.
– And writers say, as the most forward bud
Is eaten by the canker ere it blow,
Even so by love the young and tender wit
Is turned to folly, blasting in the bud,
Losing his verdure even in the prime
And all the fair effects of future hopes.

The Two Gentlemen of Verona, i.1.

[This statement is of prime autobiographical significance, for Shakespeare is referring to himself in 'when writers say' – it is he who says precisely this in Sonnets 33–35, the canker in the bud, and all. The theme of the play is the conflict between two friends for the love of one woman, i.e. between the poet and his young patron over Emilia Lanier. Thus 'the finest wits of all' – and there we have Shakespeare's real opinion of himself – may be consumed by love; while young Southampton may be made a fool of, losing the freshness of his youth and dimming the hopes of his future. The year is 1592.]

To be in love, where scorn is bought with groans,
Coy looks with heart-sore sighs; one fading moment's mirth
With twenty watchful, weary, tedious nights:
If haply won, perhaps a hapless gain;
If lost, why then a grievous labour won:
However, but a folly bought with wit,
Or else a wit by folly vanquishèd.

The Two Gentlemen of Verona, i.1.

31

[This was precisely Shakespeare's experience at the hands of his dark young lady at this precise time, 1592; again the language has its parallels, both in the Sonnets and in *The Rape of Lucrece*. They all corroborate each other – this is no general reflection, but the writer's own experience. The Elizabethans by 'wit' meant intelligence; *cf.* Sonnet 140, 'If I might teach thee wit' – how revealing of what attracted the younger woman in the older man!]

> Who by repentance is not satisfied
> Is nor of heaven nor earth, for these are pleased.
> By penitence the Eternal's wrath's appeased:
> And that my love may appear plain and free,
> All that was mine in Silvia I give thee.
> *The Two Gentlemen of Verona*, v.4.

[All 'critics' have found this *dénouement* of the conflict between friendship and love – the subject of this play – in which one friend hands over his girl to the other offending friend, as unreal, improbable. It is in fact what happened between the writer and his young patron: 'Take all my loves, my love, yea take them all.' Note the emphasis on penitence, and the young patron's 'repentance' in the Sonnets. The play reflects the contemporaneous experience.]

>   . . . a merrier man,
> Within the limit of becoming mirth,
> I never spent an hoür's talk withal.
> His eye begets occasion for his wit;
> For every object that the one doth catch
> The other turns to a mirth-moving jest:
> Which his fair tongue, conceit's expositor,
> Delivers in such apt and gracious words
> That agèd ears play truant at his tales,
> And younger hearings are quite ravishèd,
> So sweet and voluble is his discourse.
> *Love's Labour's Lost*, ii.1.

[In this skit on the Southampton circle its poet is laughing at himself, and his characteristics, in the character of Berowne.]

>   . . . to live and study here three years –
> But there are other strict observances –

As, not to see a woman in that term,
Which I hope well is not enrollèd there!
And one day in a week to touch no food,
And but one meal on every day beside –
The which I hope is not enrollèd there!
And then, to sleep but three hours in the night,
And not to be seen to wink of all the day –
When I was wont to think no harm all night,
And make a dark night too of half the day:
Which I hope well is not enrollèd there!

Love's Labour's Lost, i.1.

Why, all delights are vain; but that most vain
Which, with pain purchased, doth inherit pain:
As, painfully to pore upon a book
To seek the light of truth: while truth the while
Doth falsely blind the eyesight of his look.
Light seeking light doth light of light beguile –
So, ere you find where light in darkness lies,
Your light grows dark by losing of your eyes.
Study me how to please the eye indeed
By fixing it upon a fairer eye,
Who, dazzling so, that eye shall be his heed,
And give him light that it was blinded by.

Study is like the heaven's glorious sun,
That will not be deep-searched with saucy looks;
Small have continual plodders ever won,
Save base authority from others' books.
Those earthly godfathers of heaven's lights
That give a name to every fixèd star,
Have no more profit of their shining nights
Than those that walk and wot not what they are.
Too much to know is to know naught but fame;
And every godfather can give a name.

Love's Labour's Lost, i.1.

From women's eyes this doctrine I derive:
They sparkle still [ever] the right Promethean fire;
They are the books, the arts, the academes,
That show, contain, and nourish all the world.

Love's Labour's Lost, iv.3.

Not from the stars do I my judgment pluck,
And yet methinks I have astronomy,
But not to tell of good or evil luck,
Of plagues, of dearths, or seasons' quality;
Nor can I fortune to brief minutes tell,
Pointing to each his thunder, rain and wind,
Or say with princes if it shall go well,
By oft predict that I in heaven find.

Sonnet 14

Let those who are in favour with their stars
Of public honour and proud titles boast,
Whilst I, whom fortune of such triumph bars,
Unlooked for joy in that I honour most.

Sonnet 25

[Several times he expresses his resentment at his lot in life – naturally, with such ambition, self-confidence, and pretensions to gentility – all thoroughly justified.]

When in disgrace with fortune and men's eyes,
I all alone beweep my outcast state,
And trouble deaf heaven with my bootless cries,
And look upon myself, and curse my fate:
Wishing me like to one more rich in hope,
Featured like him, like him with friends possessed,
Desiring this man's art and that man's scope,
With what I most enjoy contented least.

Sonnet 29

When to the sessions of sweet silent thought
I summon up remembrance of things past,
I sigh the lack of many a thing I sought
And with old woes new wail my dear time's waste:
Then can I drown an eye, unused to flow,
For precious friends hid in death's dateless night,
And weep afresh love's long since cancelled woe,
And moan the expense of many a vanished sight:
Then can I grieve at grievances foregone,
And heavily from woe to woe tell o'er
The sad account of fore-bemoanèd moan,
Which I new pay as if not paid before.

Sonnet 30

And all those friends which I thought burièd . . .
How many a holy and obsequious tear
Hath dear religious love stolen from mine eye,
As interest of the dead . . .

Sonnet 31

Sin of self-love possesseth all mine eye,
And all my soul, and all my every part;
And for this sin there is no remedy,
It is so grounded inward in my heart.
Methinks no face so gracious is as mine,
No shape so true, no truth of such account;
And for myself mine own worth do define
As I all others in all worths surmount.
But when my glass shows me myself indeed,
Beated and chopped with tanned antiquity,
Mine own self-love quite contrary I read:
Self, so self-loving, were iniquity.

Sonnet 62

Against my love shall be, as I am now,
With Time's injurious hand crushed and o'erworn.

Sonnet 63

No longer mourn for me when I am dead
Than you shall hear the surly sullen bell
Give warning to the world that I am fled
From this vile world with vilest worms to dwell:
Nay, if you read this line, remember not
The hand that writ it; for I love you so
That I in your sweet thoughts would be forgot
If thinking on me then should make you woe.
O if, I say, you look upon this verse
When I perhaps compounded am with clay,
Do not so much as my poor name rehearse,
But let your love even with my life decay.

Sonnet 71

O, lest the world should task you to recite
What merit lived in me that you should love,
After my death, dear love, forget me quite,

For you in me can nothing worthy prove . . .
For I am shamed by that which I bring forth,
And so should you, to love things nothing worth.

Sonnet 72

That time of year thou mayst in me behold
When yellow leaves, or none, or few, do hang . . .
In me thou see'st the glowing of such fire
That on the ashes of his youth doth lie . . .
Consumed with that which it was nourished by.

Sonnet 73

My life hath in this line some interest,
Which for memorial still with thee shall stay.
When thou reviewest this, thou dost review
The very part was consecrate to thee:
The earth can have but earth, which is his due,
My spirit is thine, the better part of me.

Sonnet 74

Or shall I live your epitaph to make,
Or you survive when I in earth am rotten . . .
The earth can yield me but a common grave,
When you entombèd in men's eyes shall lie.
Your monument shall be my gentle verse.

Sonnet 81

[It has been observed that this coincides with the date of the contract for
the magnificent Southampton tomb in Titchfield church, 1593, upon
which the patron appears as a boy on the side. And we observe
frequently Shakespeare's express notice of monuments, so characteristic
a feature of the age.]

When thou shalt be disposed to set me light
And place my merit in the eye of scorn,
Upon thy side against myself I'll fight . . .
With mine own weakness being best acquainted,
Upon thy part I can set down a story
Of faults concealed, wherein I am attainted.

Sonnet 88

Say that thou didst forsake me for some fault,
And I will comment upon that offence;
Speak of my lameness, and I straight will halt,
Against thy reasons making no defence.
Thou canst not, love, disgrace me half so ill,
To set a form upon desirèd change,
As I'll myself disgrace: knowing thy will,
I will acquaintance strangle and look strange;
Be absent from thy walks . . .

Sonnet 89

Then hate me when thou wilt; if ever, now:
Now while the world is bent my deeds to cross,
Join with the spite of fortune, make me bow,
And do not drop in for an after-loss . . .
If thou wilt leave me, do not leave me last,
When other petty griefs have done their spite,
But in the onset come: so shall I taste
At first the very worst of fortune's might.

Sonnet 90

Thy love is better than high birth to me,
Richer than wealth, prouder than garments' cost,
Of more delight than hawks or horses be;
And having thee of all men's pride I boast.

Sonnet 91

But do thy worst to steal thyself away,
For term of life thou art assurèd mine,
And life no longer than thy love will stay,
For it depends upon that love of thine.
Then need I not to fear the worst of wrongs,
When in the least of them my life hath end;
I see a better state to me belongs
Than that which on thy humour doth depend.
Thou canst not vex me with inconstant mind,
Since that my life on thy revolt doth lie.

Sonnet 92

How like a winter hath my absence been
From thee, the pleasure of the fleeting year!

What freezings have I felt, what dark days seen!
What old December's bareness everywhere!
And yet this time removed was summer's time,
The teeming autumn, big with rich increase,
Bearing the wanton burden of the prime.

Sonnet 97

From you I have been absent in the spring,
When proud-pied April, dressed in all his trim,
Hath put a spirit of youth in everything . . .
Yet nor the lays of birds, nor the sweet smell
Of different flowers in odour and in hue
Could make me any summer's story tell . . .

Sonnet 98

My love is strengthened, though more weak in seeming,
I love not less, though less the show appear . . .
Our love was new, and then but in the spring,
When I was wont to greet it with my lays
As Philomel in summer's front doth sing,
And stops her pipe in growth of riper days.

Sonnet 102

O, never say that I was false of heart,
Though absence seemed my flame to qualify:
As easy might I from myself depart
As from my soul, which in thy breast doth lie.
That is my home of love: if I have ranged,
Like him that travels I return again . . .
Never believe, though in my nature reigned
All frailties that besiege all kinds of blood,
That it could so preposterously be stained
To leave for nothing all thy sum of good.

Sonnet 109

Alas, 'tis true I have gone here and there,
And made myself a motley to the view,
Gored mine own thoughts, sold cheap what is most dear,
Made old offences of affections new.

Sonnet 110

[Once more we have the gentlemanly actor's resentment at the profession by which he earns his living.]

O, for my sake do you with Fortune chide,
The guilty goddess of my harmful deeds,
That did not better for my life provide
Than public means, which public manners breeds.
Thence comes it that my name receives a brand,
And almost thence my nature is subdued
To what it works in, like the dyer's hand.

Sonnet 111

Your love and pity doth the impression fill
Which vulgar scandal stamped upon my brow;
For what care I who calls me well or ill,
So you o'er-green [Greene] my bad, my good allow? . . .
In so profound abysm I throw all care
Of others' voices, that my adder's sense
To critic and to flatterer stoppèd are.

Sonnet 112

[He greatly resented Greene's insulting attack upon him in 1592; his worshipful friends stood by him, testifying to his upright character, and got a handsome apology out of the publisher.]

Let me not to the marriage of true minds
Admit impediments: love is not love
Which alters when it alteration finds,
Or bends with the remover to remove.

Sonnet 116

Accuse me thus – that I have scanted all
Wherein I should your great deserts repay,
Forgot upon your dearest love to call,
Whereto all bonds do tie me day by day;
That I have frequent been with unknown minds,
And given to time your own dear-purchased right.

Sonnet 117

[Always, everywhere he acknowledges his indebtedness to the patron, but acting takes him away from him increasingly in 1594, after the formation of the Lord Chamberlain's Company.]

Even so, being full of your ne'er cloying sweetness,
To bitter sauces did I frame my feeding,
And sick of welfare found a kind of meetness
To be diseased, ere that there was true needing.

Sonnet 118

What potions have I drunk of Siren tears
Distilled from limbecks foul as hell within,
Applying fears to hopes and hopes to fears,
Still [ever] losing when I saw myself to win!
What wretched errors hath my heart committed,
Whilst it hath thought itself so blessèd never!
How have mine eyes out of their spheres been fitted
In the distraction of this madding fever!
O benefit of ill: now I find true
That better is by evil still [ever] made better,
And ruined love, when it is built anew,
Grows fairer than at first, more strong, far greater.

Sonnet 119

For if you were by my unkindness shaken
As I by yours, you've passed a hell of time;
And I, a tyrant, have no leisure taken
To weigh how once I suffered in your crime.
O, that our night of woe might have remembered
My deepest sense, how hard true sorrow hits,
And soon to you, as you to me then, tendered
The humble salve which wounded bosoms fits!

Sonnet 120

'Tis better to be vile than vile esteemed,
When not to be receives reproach of being;
And the just pleasure lost, which is so deemed –
Not by our feeling – but by others' seeing.
For why should others' false adulterate eyes
Give salutation to my sportive blood?
Or on my frailties why are frailer spies,
Which in their wills count bad what I think good?
No, I am that I am, and they that level
At my abuses reckon up their own:
I may be straight, though they themselves be bevel,
By their rank thoughts my deeds must not be shown.

Sonnet 121

[Here we have the most candid and downright defence of himself, and his chief weakness – that of a highly sexed heterosexual for women – borne out throughout the plays.]

> They say best men are moulded out of faults,
> And, for the most part, become much more the better
> For being a little bad.
>
> *Measure for Measure*, v.1.

> The expense of spirit in a waste of shame
> Is lust in action; and till action, lust
> Is perjured, murderous, bloody, full of blame,
> Savage, extreme, rude, cruel, not to trust;
> Enjoyed no sooner but despisèd straight,
> Past reason hunted, and no sooner had
> Past reason hated, as a swallowed bait
> On purpose laid to make the taker mad,
> Mad in pursuit and in possession so,
> Had, having, and in quest to have, extreme;
> A bliss in proof and, proved, a very woe,
> Before a joy proposed, behind a dream.
>
> Sonnet 129

> No, Time thou shalt not boast that I do change.
>
> Sonnet 123

> If my dear love were but the child of state,
> It might for fortune's bastard be unfathered
> As subject to time's love or to time's hate . . .
> No, it was builded far from accident;
> It suffers not in smiling pomp, nor falls
> Under the blow of thrallèd discontent
> Whereto the inviting time our fashion calls:
> It fears not policy, that heretic,
> Which works on leases of short-numbered hours,
> But all alone stands hugely politic,
> That it nor grows with heat nor drowns with showers.
>
> Sonnet 124

[The images reflect the date – a crest in the persecution of seminary priests and Jesuits in the winter of 1594–5.]

Were it aught to me I bore the canopy,
With my extern the outward honouring . . .
Have I not seen dwellers on form and favour
Lose all and more by paying too much rent . . .
Pitiful thrivers in their gazing spent?
No, let me be obsequious in thy heart,
And take thou my oblation poor but free,
Which is not mixed with seconds, knows no art
But mutual render, only me for thee.

Sonnet 125

[This concludes the Southampton sequence, which began with reiterated assurance of duty to the young patron – 'Lord of my love', etc, and now ends with a fine assertion of equality – inner equality of spirit – for all his external duty, bearing 'the canopy' for a 'child of state', the adolescent Earl. For all his resentment at having to earn his living by the theatre, it gave him independence and shortly won him the status of an armigerous gentleman, eventually a sufficient fortune for his family.]

Gentility

ȝ

I am a gentleman of blood and breeding.

King Lear, III.1.

He is complete in feature and in mind
With all good grace to grace a gentleman.
The Two Gentlemen of Verona, II.4.

Here is newly come to Court . . . an absolute gentleman, full of most
excellent differences [qualities], of very soft society and great
showing . . . he is the card or calendar of gentry, for you shall find in
him the continent of what part a gentleman would see.

Hamlet, v.2.

My father charged you in his will to give me good education: you
have trained me like a peasant, obscuring and hiding from me all
gentleman-like qualities . . .
It was upon this fashion bequeathed me by will but poor a thousand
crowns and . . . charged my brother to breed me well . . . Call you
that keeping for a gentleman of my birth, that differs not from the
stalling of an ox? His horses are bred better, for they are taught their
manage, and to that end riders dearly hired . . . He lets me feed with
his hinds, bars me the place of a brother and mines my gentility with
my education.

As You Like It, I.1.

I know a discontented gentleman,
Whose humble means match not his haughty mind.
Richard III, IV.2.

43

Leaving me no sign,
Save men's opinions and my living blood
To show the world I am a gentleman.

Richard II, iii.1.

He's a yeoman that has a gentleman to his son; for he's a mad yeoman that sees his son a gentleman before him.

King Lear, iii.6.

[When Shakespeare took out a coat-of-arms, he took it out in his father's name, so that himself was a gentleman born. Ben Jonson laughed at this, and the motto *Non sans droict* – not without right – and suggested for crest a boar's head, for motto 'Not without mustard'.]

If you strike me, you are no gentleman;
And if no gentleman, why then no arms.

The Taming of the Shrew, ii.1.

When a gentleman is disposed to swear, it is not for any standers-by to curtail his oaths.

Cymbeline, ii.1.

[This may be cocking a snook at those in Parliament forwarding an Act against Profanity in 1605–6; play texts reveal censorship of oaths in them, interference hardly likely to be appreciated by writers.]

Then you must undertake to slander him
– 'Tis an ill office for a gentleman,
Especially against his very friend.

The Two Gentlemen of Verona, iii.2.

As I am a gentleman.
– Faith, you said so before.
As I am a gentleman!

2 Henry IV, ii.1.

As you are certainly a gentleman, thereto clerkly-experienced – which no less adorns our gentry than our parents' noble names, in whose success[ion] we are gentle.

The Winter's Tale, i.2.

['Clerkly-experienced', e.g. university graduates as such qualified for the
status of 'gentleman'; *cf.* Sir Thomas Smith, *De Republica Anglorum*.
Shakespeare did not have this qualification, unlike Marlowe and the
university wits – all the more reason to emphasise his better birth.]

> We marry
> A gentler scion to the wildest stock,
> And make conceive a bark of baser kind
> By bud of nobler race. This is an art
> Which does mend nature – change it rather – but
> The art itself is nature.
>
> *The Winter's Tale*, iv.4.

A most lovely gentleman-like man.

A Midsummer Night's Dream, i.2.

Theatre

Shall we have a play of this?

Cymbeline, v.5.

How many ages hence
Shall this our lofty scene be acted over,
In states unborn, and accents yet unknown?

Julius Caesar, iii.1.

This wide and universal theatre
Presents more woeful pageants than the scene
Wherein we play in . . .
All the world's a stage,
And all the men and women merely players;
They have their exits and their entrances,
And one man in his time plays many parts,
His acts being seven ages.

As You Like It, ii.7.

Hung be the heavens [upper stage] with black!

1 Henry VI, i.1.

Black stage for tragedies and murders fell.

The Rape of Lucrece

As if the tragedy
Were played by counterfeiting actors.

3 Henry VI, ii.3.

Speak . . . it is your cue.

Much Ado About Nothing, ii.1.

Remember your cue
– I warrant you. If I do not act it, hiss me.

The Merry Wives of Windsor, III.3.

When Roscius was an actor in Rome –

Hamlet, II.2.

What scene of death hath Roscius now to act?

3 Henry VI, V.6.

[Roscius, most famous of Roman actors, was a great name with Elizabethan theatre folk, especially the professional Shakespeare, always ready to display his classical knowledge.]

Methinks I play as I have seen them do
In Whitsun pastorals: sure this robe of mine
Does change my disposition.

The Winter's Tale, IV.3.

We'll have no Cupid hoodwinked with a scarf,
Bearing a Tartar's painted bow of lath . . .
Nor no without-book Prologue, faintly spoke
After the Prompter, for our entrance.

Romeo and Juliet, I.4.

Our wooing doth not end like an old play:
Jack hath not Jill; these ladies' courtesy
Might well have made our sport a comedy.

Love's Labour's Lost, V.2.

If we shadows have offended
Think but this and all is mended,
That you have but slumbered here,
While these visions did appear,
And this weak and idle theme,
No more yielding but a dream,
Gentles, do not reprehend:
If you pardon, we will mend.
And as I'm an honest Puck,
If we have unearnèd luck
Now to scape the serpent's tongue,

We will make amends ere long:
Else the Puck a liar call.
So, good night unto you all.

A Midsummer Night's Dream, v.2.

By heavens, these scroyles [wretches] of Angiers flout you, kings,
And stand securely on their battlements
As in a theatre, whence they gape and point
At your industrious scenes and acts of death.

King John, ii.1.

Two households, both alike in dignity,
In fair Verona, where we lay our scene,
From ancient grudge break to new mutiny . . .
Is now the two hours' traffic of our stage:
The which if you with patient ears attend,
What here shall miss our toil shall strive to mend.

Romeo and Juliet, Prologue

I see the play so lies
That I must bear a part.

The Winter's Tale, iv.4.

And let this world no longer be a stage
To feed contention in a lingering act.

2 Henry IV, i.1.

It is not the fashion to see the lady the Epilogue; but it is no more unhandsome than to see the lord the Prologue. If it be true that good wine needs no bush, 'tis true that a good play needs no Epilogue. Yet to good wine they do use good bushes, and good plays prove the better by good Epilogues.

What a case am I in then, that am neither a good Epilogue, nor cannot insinuate with you in the behalf of a good play! I am not furnished like a beggar, therefore to beg will not become me: my way is to conjure you, and I'll begin with the women.

I charge you, O women, for the love you bear to men, to like as much of this play as please you. And I charge you, O men, for the love you bear to women – as I perceive by your simpering none of you hate them – that between you and the women the play may please.

If I were a woman I would kiss as many of you as had beards that pleased me, complexions that liked me, and breaths that I defied not. And I am sure, as many as have good beards, or good faces, or sweet breaths, will, for my kind offer, when I make curtsy, bid me farewell.

As You Like It, Epilogue

First, my fear; then, my curtsy; last, my speech. My fear is your displeasure; my curtsy my duty; and my speech to beg your pardon. If you look for a good speech now you undo me; for what I have to say is of mine own making. And what indeed I should say, will, I doubt [fear], prove mine own marring.

But to the purpose, and so to the venture.

Be it known to you – as it is very well – I was lately here in the end of a displeasing play, to pray your patience for it and to promise you a better. I did mean indeed to pay you with this; which, if like an ill venture it come unluckily home, I break, and you, my gentle creditors, lose.

Here, I promised you I would be, and here I commit my body to your mercies. Bate [abate] me some and I will pay you some; and as most debtors do, promise you infinitely . . .

All the gentlewomen here have forgive men; if the gentlemen will not, then the gentlemen will not agree with the gentlewomen, which was never seen before in such an assembly.

One word more, I beseech you. If you be not too much cloyed with fat meat, our humble author will continue the story, with Sir John in it, and make you merry with fair Katherine of France. Where, for anything I know, Falstaff shall die of a sweat, unless already 'a be killed with your hard opinions; for Oldcastle died a martyr, and this is not the man.

My tongue is weary; when my legs are too, I will bid you goodnight, and so kneel down before you, but, indeed, to pray for the Queen.

2 Henry IV, Epilogue

But pardon, gentles all,
The flat unraisèd spirits that hath dared
On this unworthy scaffold to bring forth
So great an object. Can this cockpit hold
The vasty fields of France? Or may we cram
Within this wooden O the very casques

That did affright the air at Agincourt?
O pardon! since a crooked figure may
Attest in little place a million;
And let us, ciphers in this great account,
On your imaginary forces work.

Suppose within the girdle of these walls
Are now confined two mighty monarchies,
Whose high uprearèd and abutting fronts
The perilous narrow ocean parts asunder.
Piece out our imperfections with your thoughts:
Into a thousand parts divide one man,
And make imaginary puïssance.
Think when we talk of horses that you see them
Printing their proud hoofs in the receiving earth.
For 'tis your thoughts that now must deck our kings,
Carry them here and there, jumping o'er times,
Turning the accomplishment of many years
Into an hour-glass. For the which supply,
Admit me Chorus to this history:
Who Prologue-like your humble patience pray,
Gently to hear, kindly to judge, our play.

Henry V, i. Chorus

       . . . the scene
Is now transported, gentles, to Southampton.
There is the playhouse now, there must you sit;
And thence to France shall we convey you safe,
And bring you back, charming the narrow seas
To give you gentle pass. For, if we may,
We'll not offend one stomach with our play.
But, till the King come forth and not till then,
Unto Southampton do we shift our scene.

Henry V, ii. Chorus

      . . . Suppose that you have seen
The well-appointed King at Hampton pier
Embark his royalty; and his brave fleet
With silken streamers the young Phoebus fanning.
Play with your fancies, and in them behold
Upon the hempen tackle shipboys climbing;
Hear the shrill whistle which doth order give

To sounds confused. Behold the threaden sails
Borne with the invisible and creeping wind,
Draw the huge bottoms through the furrowed sea,
Breasting the lofty surge. O, do but think
You stand upon the rivage and behold
A city upon the inconstant billows dancing . . .
         . . . Follow, follow!
Grapple your minds to sternage of this navy . . .
Work, work your thoughts, and therein see a siege.
         . . . Still [ever] be kind,
And eke out our performance with your mind.

Henry V, iii. Chorus

         . . . Then mean and gentle all,
Behold, as may unworthiness define,
A little touch of Harry in the night.
And so our scene must to the battle fly:
Where – O, for pity – we shall much disgrace,
With four or five most vile and ragged foils [swords],
Right ill-disposed and brawl ridiculous,
The name of Agincourt. Yet sit and see,
Minding true things by what their mockeries be.

Henry V, iv. Chorus

Vouchsafe to those that have not read the story
That I may prompt them; and of such as have
I humbly pray them to admit the excuse
Of time, of numbers, and due course of things,
Which cannot in their huge and proper life
Be here presented . . .
         Myself have played
The interim, by remembering you 'tis past.
Then brook abridgement, and your eyes advance
After your thoughts straight back again to France.

Henry V, v. Chorus

Thus far, with rough and all-unable pen,
Our bending author hath pursued the story;
In little room confining mighty men,
Mangling by starts the full course of their glory.
Small time, but in that small most greatly lived
This star of England . . .

Henry the Sixth, in infant bands crowned King
Of France and England, did this King succeed;
Whose state so many had the managing
That they lost France and made his England bleed.
Which oft our stage hath shown. And, for their sake,
In your fair minds let this acceptance take.

Henry V, Epilogue

[This, 'our bending author', would indicate that Shakespeare himself spoke the Epilogue, and Chorus, bowing courteously to the audience. Opportunity should be taken in productions to bring him back on the stage as himself.]

I, that please some, try all, both joy and terror
Of good and bad, that make and unfold error,
Now take upon me, in the name of Time,
To use my wings. Impute it not a crime
To me or my swift passage, that I slide
O'er sixteen years, and leave the growth untried
Of that wide gap. Since it is in my power
To o'erthrow law, and in one self-born hour
To plant and o'erwhelm custom. Let me pass
The same I am, ere ancient'st order was
Or what is now received. I witness to
The times that brought them in; so shall I do
To the freshest things now reigning, and make stale
The glistering of this present, as my tale
Now seems to it. Your patience this allowing,
I turn my glass and give my scene such growing
As you had slept between . . .
              Of this allow,
If ever you have spent time worse ere now:
If never, yet that Time himself doth say
He wishes earnestly you never may.

The Winter's Tale, IV. Chorus

If the tag-rag people did not clap him and hiss him, according as he pleased and displeased them, as they use to do in the theatre.

Julius Caesar, I.2.

. . . now the play is done:
All is well ended if this suit be won
That you express content: which we will pay
With strife to please you, day exceeding day.
Ours be your patience then, and yours our parts;
Your gentle hands lend us, and take our hearts.

All's Well That Ends Well, Epilogue

. . . Hither am I come
A Prologue armed, but not in confidence
Of author's pen or actor's voice, but suited
In like conditions as our argument[1] –
To tell you, fair beholders, that our play
Leaps o'er the vaunt and firstlings of those broils,
Beginning in the middle; starting thence away
To what may be digested in a play.
Like or find fault; do as your pleasures are:
Now good or bad, 'tis but the chance of war.

Troilus and Cressida, Prologue

To sing a song that old was sung,
From ashes ancient Gower is come,
Assuming man's infirmities,
To glad your ear and please your eyes . . .
What now ensues to the judgment of your eye
I give, my cause who best can justify.

Pericles, i. Chorus

[The poet Gower appears as Chorus throughout *Pericles*. Note that his tomb, with effigy and his book, the *Confessio Amantis* – the source of the play – was a dominant feature in St Mary Overy church (now Southwark cathedral), near the Globe Theatre. And that Shakespeare was much given to noticing monuments.]

. . . What ensues in this fell storm
Shall for itself itself perform.

[1] This is Shakespeare's riposte to Ben Jonson, who in *The Poetaster* in 1601 had brought on Prologue Armed 'in well-erected confidence' against his opponents. Jonson had started the theatre war, Boys' versus Men's Companies. Shakespeare's reproof reminds Ben, next year, to stick rather to the argument of the play.

I nill relate, action may
Conveniently the rest convey,
Which might not what by me is told.
In your imagination hold
This stage the ship, upon whose deck
The sea-tossed Pericles appears to speak.

Pericles, iii. Chorus

. . . The unborn event
I do commend to your content.
Only I carry wingèd time
Post on the lame feet of my rhyme:
Which never could I so convey
Unless your thoughts went on my way.

Pericles, iv. Chorus

Thus time we waste, and long leagues make short,
Sail seas in cockles, have and wish but for't,
Working to take your imagination
From bourn to bourn, region to region.
By you being pardoned, we commit no crime
To use one language in each several clime
Where our scene seems to live . . .
Like motes and shadows see them move awhile:
Your ears unto your eyes I'll reconcile.

Pericles, iv.4. Chorus

In your supposing once more put your sight
Of heavy Pericles: think that his bark:
Where what is done in action, more, if might,
Shall be discovered. Please you, sit and hark.

Pericles, v. Chorus

So on your patience evermore attending,
New joy wait on you! Here our play hath ending.

Pericles, Epilogue

I come no more to make you laugh: things now,
That bear a weighty and a serious brow,
Sad, high and working, full of state and woe,
Such noble scenes as draw the eye to flow,

We now present. Those that can pity, here
May, if they think it well, let fall a tear –
The subject will deserve it. Such as give
Their money out of hope they may believe
May here find truth too. Those that come to see
Only a show or two, and so agree
The play may pass, if they be still and willing,
I'll undertake may see away their shilling
Richly in two short hours. Only they
That come to hear a merry, bawdy play,
A noise of targets, or to see a fellow
In a long, motley coat guarded with yellow,
Will be deceived. For, gentle hearers, know,
To rank our chosen truth with such a show
As fool and fight is, besides forfeiting
Our own brains and the opinion that we bring,
To make that only true we now intend,
Will leave us never an understanding friend.

Therefore, for goodness' sake, and as you are known,
The first and happiest hearers of the town,
Be sad as we would make ye. Think ye see
The very persons of our noble story
As they were living. Think you see them great,
And followed with the general throng and sweat
Of thousand friends. Then in a moment see
How soon this mightiness meets misery.
And if you can be merry then, I'll say
A man may weep upon his wedding day.

Henry VIII, Prologue

'Tis ten to one this play can never please
All that are here. Some come to take their ease
And sleep an act or two. But those we fear
We frighted with our trumpets – so 'tis clear
They'll say 'tis naught. Others to hear the city
Abused extremely and to cry, 'That's witty.'
Which we have not done neither. That I fear
All the expected good we're like to hear
For this play at this time is only in
The merciful construction of good women.

For such a one we showed 'em; if they smile
And say 'twill do, I know, within a while
All the best men are ours. For 'tis ill hap
If they hold when their ladies bid 'em clap.

Henry VIII, Epilogue

Our revels now are ended. These our actors,
As I foretold you, were all spirits and
Are melted into air, into thin air.
And, like the baseless fabric of this vision,
The cloud-capped towers, the gorgeous palaces,
The solemn temples, the great globe itself –
Yea, all which it inherit – shall dissolve,
And like this insubstantial pageant faded,
Leave not a rack behind. We are such stuff
As dreams are made on, and our little life
Is rounded with a sleep.

The Tempest, iv.1.

Actors and Acting

ะ

As in a theatre the eyes of men,
After a well-graced actor leaves the stage,
Are idly bent on him that enters next,
Thinking his prattle to be tedious.

Richard II, v.2.

As an unperfect actor on the stage
Who with his fear is put beside his part,
Or some fierce thing replete with too much rage
Whose strength's abundance weakens his own heart.

Sonnet 23

    Like a dull actor now
I have forgot my part, and I am out,
Even to a full disgrace.

Coriolanus, v.3.

Like a strutting player, whose conceit
Lies in his hamstring, and doth think it rich
To hear the wooden dialogue and sound
Twixt his stretched footing and the scaffoldage.

Troilus and Cressida, i.3.

Thou, an Egyptian puppet, shall be shown
In Rome as well as I . . .
    The quick comedians
Extemporally will stage us, and present

Our Alexandrian revels. Antony
Shall be brought drunken forth, and I shall see
Some squeaking Cleopatra boy my greatness
In the posture of a whore.

Antony and Cleopatra, v.2.

He that plays the king shall be welcome; the adventurous knight
shall use his foil [sword] and target [shield]; the lover shall not sigh
gratis; the humorous man shall end his part in peace; the clown
shall make those laugh whose lungs are tickle o' the sere [easily
tickled]; and the lady shall say her mind freely, or the blank verse
shall halt for it. What players are they? . . .

How chances it they travel? Their residence, both in reputation
and profit, was better both ways.

– I think their inhibition comes by the means of the late innovation.

Do they hold the same estimation they did? . . . Are they so
followed?

– No, indeed they are not.

How comes it? Do they grow rusty?

– Nay, their endeavour keeps in the wonted pace. But there is an
eyrie of children, little eyases, that cry out on the top of question and
are most tyrannically clapped for it. These are now the fashion, and
so berattle the common stages – so they call them – that many
wearing rapiers are afraid of goose quills, and dare scarce come
thither.

What! Are they children? Who maintains 'em? How are they
escoted [supported]? Will they pursue the quality no longer than
they can sing? Will they not say afterwards, if they should grow to
common players – as it is most like, if their means are no better –
their writers do them wrong, to exclaim against their own
succession?

– Faith, there has been much to-do on both sides; and the nation
holds it no sin to tarre [incite] them to controversy. There was for a
while no money bid for argument unless the poet and the player
went to cuffs in the question.

– O, there has been much throwing about of brains.

Do the boys carry it away?

– Ay, that they do: Hercules and his load too.

Hamlet, ii.2.

[Fascinating autobiographically, and for contemporary stage history. These years 1600–1 saw a rivalry between the Men's Companies and the Boys', rising to warfare started by Ben Jonson writing for the latter, and Marston and Dekker for the Men's. The heated controversy was good business, as we see from Shakespeare's comment, mild in the circumstances, though going to the point – so like him, to be not personally offensive, unlike Jonson, who recognised this gentlemanliness in his senior. All the same, we note a touch of resentment in his reference to his own side, 'the common stages, so they call them . . . common players'. 'Hercules and his load', the globe, was the sign of Shakespeare's theatre, the Globe, losing custom for a time. 'The late innovation' may refer to Essex's rising of February 1601 in the City – an innocuous way of referring to the event. One should notice his characteristically uncontroversial way of referring to these events, in rather general terms, not engaging in the controversy himself. The Boys' 'writers' would be doing them wrong to attack the adult stage they might need when grown up: this meant Jonson, harmlessly enough, whom Shakespeare had given his chance at the Globe and acted in one of his plays there. Ben recognised somewhat ruefully later:

> Now for the players, it is true I taxed 'em . . .
> Only amongst them I am sorry for
> Some better natures by the rest so drawn
> To run in that vile line.]

Hamlet: Come, give us a taste of your quality; come, a passionate speech.
First Player: What speech, my good lord?
Hamlet: I heard thee speak me a speech once, but it was never acted; or, if it was, not above once. For the play, I remember, pleased not the million: 'twas caviare to the general. But it was – as I received it, and others whose judgment in such matters cried in the top of mine – an excellent play, well digested in the scenes, set down with as much modesty as cunning. I remember one said there were no sallets [sallies] in the lines to make the matter savoury; nor no matter in the phrase that might indict the author of affectation. But [he] called it an honest method, as wholesome as sweet, and by very much more handsome than fine. One speech in it I chiefly loved: 'twas Aeneas' tale to Dido; and thereabout of it specially, where he speaks of Priam's slaughter. If it live in your memory, begin at this line; let me see, let me see . . .

Polonius: This is too long.

Hamlet: It shall to the barber's, with your beard. Prithee, say on; he's for a jig or a tale of bawdry, or he sleeps. Say on; come to Hecuba . . .

Polonius: Look, whether he has not turned his colour and has tears in his eyes. Prithee, no more.

Hamlet: 'Tis well. I'll have thee speak out the rest soon. Good my lord, will you see the players well bestowed? Do you hear, let them be well used; for they are the abstracts and brief chronicles of the time. After your death, you were better have a bad epitaph than their ill report while you live.

Ibid.

Polonius: The best actors in the world, either for tragedy, comedy, history, pastoral, pastoral-comical, historical-pastoral, tragical-historical, tragical-comical-historical-pastoral; scene individable, or poem unlimited – Seneca cannot be too heavy, nor Plautus too light. For the law of writ and the liberty, these are the only men.

Hamlet: O, Jephthah, judge of Israel, what a treasure hadst thou!

Ibid.

Speak the speech, I pray you, as I pronounced it to you – trippingly on the tongue. But if you mouth it, as many of your players do, I had as lief the town-crier spake my lines. Nor do not saw the air too much with your hand – thus. But use all gently, for in the very torrent, tempest and, as I may say, whirlwind of your passion, you must acquire and beget a temperance, that may give it smoothness.

O, it offends me to the soul to hear a robustious periwig-pated fellow tear a passion to tatters, to very rags, to split the ears of the groundlings – who for the most part are capable of nothing but inexplicable dumb-shows and noise. I would have such a fellow whipped for o'er-doing Termagant: it out-Herods Herod. Pray you, avoid it.

Hamlet, iii.1.

Be not too tame, neither. But let your own discretion be your tutor. Suit the action to the word, the word to the action. With this special observance – that you o'er-step not the modesty of nature. For anything so overdone is from the purpose of playing – whose end, both at the first and now, was and is to hold (as 'twere) the mirror up to nature; to show virtue her own feature, scorn her own image, and the very age and body of the time his form and pressure.

Now, this overdone or come tardy off, though it make the unskilful laugh, cannot but make the judicious grieve: the censure of which one must in your allowance o'erweigh a whole theatre of others.

O, there be players that I have seen play and heard others praise, and that highly, not to speak it profanely, that – neither having the accent of Christians, nor the gait of Christian, pagan, nor man – have so strutted and bellowed that I have thought some of nature's journeymen had made men and not made them well, they imitated humanity so abominably.

. . . I hope we have reformed that indifferently [fairly well] with us . . .

O, reform it altogether. And let those that play your clowns speak no more than is set down for them. For there be of them that will themselves laugh, to set on some quantity of barren spectators to laugh too – though in the meantime some necessary question of the play be then to be considered. That's villainous, and shows a most pitiful ambition in the fool that uses it.

Hamlet, III.2.

Enter Players.
Lord: Now, fellows, you are welcome.
Players: We thank your honour.
Lord: Do you intend to stay with me tonight?
A Player: So please your lordship to accept our duty.
Lord: With all my heart. This fellow I remember
Since once he played a farmer's eldest son –
'Twas where you wooed the gentlewoman so well.
I have forgot your name; but, sure, that part
Was aptly fitted and naturally performed.
A Player: I think 'twas Soto that your honour means.
Lord: 'Tis very true, thou didst it excellent.
Well, you are come to me in happy time,
The rather for I have some sport in hand
Wherein your cunning can assist me much.
There is a lord will hear you play tonight;
But I am doubtful of your modesties,
Lest, over-eyeing of his odd behaviour –
For yet his honour never heard a play –
You break into some merry passion,
And so offend him . . .

A Player: Fear not, my lord; we can contain ourselves
Were he the veriest antick [buffoon] in the world.
Lord: Go, sirrah, take them to the buttery,
And give them friendly welcome, every one:
Let them want nothing that my house affords.

The Taming of the Shrew, Induction, 1.

A Midsummer Night's Dream

The 'rude mechanicals' ' play: Quince's Prologue

If we offend it is with our good will.
That you should think we come not to offend
But with good will. To show our simple skill
That is the true beginning of our end.
Consider then we come but in despite.
We do not come as minding to content you,
Our true intent is. All for your delight
We are not here. That you should here repent you
The actors are at hand; and by their show
You shall know all that you are like to know.

*   *   *

Quince: Is all our company here?
Bottom: You were best to call them generally, man by man, according to the scrip.
Quince: Here is the roll of every man's name which is thought fit through all Athens to play in our interlude before the Duke and Duchess, on his wedding day at night.
Bottom: First, good Peter Quince, say what the play treats on; then read the names of the actors; and so grow to a point.
Quince: Marry, our play is 'The most lamentable comedy and most cruel death of Pyramus and Thisbe.'
Bottom: A very good piece of work, I assure you, and a merry. Now, good Peter Quince, call forth your actors by the scroll.

*   *   *

Quince: Masters, here are your parts; and I am to entreat you, request you, and desire you to con them by tomorrow night. And meet me in the palace wood, a mile without the town, by moonlight. There will we rehearse; for if we meet in the city, we shall be dogged with company, and our devices known. In the meantime I will draw a bill of properties such as our play wants. I pray you fail me not.

Bottom: We will meet, and there we may rehearse most obscenely and courageously. Take pains: be perfect. Adieu!

A Midsummer Night's Dream, I.2.

Bottom: Are we all met?

Quince: Pat, pat; and here's a marvellous convenient place for our rehearsal. This green plot shall be our stage, this hawthorn-brake our tiring-house; and we will do it in action, as we will do it before the Duke.

A Midsummer Night's Dream, III.1.

Bottom (waking): When my cue comes, call me and I will answer. My next is, 'Most fair Pyramus.' Heigh-ho! Peter Quince? Flute, the bellows mender? Snout the tinker? Starveling? God's my life! Stolen hence, and left me asleep!

A Midsummer Night's Dream, IV.1.

Philostrate, Master of the Revels: A play there is some ten words long,
Which is as brief as I have known a play.
But by ten words, my lord, it is too long,
Which makes it tedious; for in all the play
There is not one word apt, one player fitted.
And tragical, my noble lord, it is
For Pyramus therein doth kill himself –
Which, when I saw rehearsed, I must confess
Made mine eyes water; but more merry tears
The passion of loud laughter never shed.
Theseus: What are they that do play it?
Philo.: Hard-handed men that work in Athens here,
Which never laboured in their minds till now;
And now have toiled their unbreathed memories
With this same play against your nuptials . . .
Theseus: I will hear that play;
For never anything can come amiss
When simpleness and duty tender it.
Go, bring them in; and take your places, ladies . . .
Philo.: So please your grace the Prologue is addressed . . .
Theseus: This fellow doth not stand upon points.
Lysander: He hath rid his prologue like a rough colt; he knows not the stop . . .
Hippolyta: Indeed he hath played on this prologue like a child on a recorder: a sound, but not in government.

Theseus: The Wall, methinks, being sensible, should curse again.
Bottom (speaking out of his part): No, in truth sir, he should not. 'Deceiving me' is Thisbe's cue: she is to enter now, and I am to spy her through the wall. You shall see it will fall pat as I told you. Yonder she comes . . .
Theseus: Now is the mure razed between the two neighbours . . .
Hippolyta: This is the silliest stuff that ever I heard.
Theseus: The best in this kind are but shadows; and the worst are no worse, if imagination amend them.

A Midsummer Night's Dream, v.1.

Here is like to be a good presence of Worthies. He presents Hector of Troy; the swain, Pompey the Great; the parish curate, Alexander; Armado's page, Hercules; the pedant, Judas Maccabeus. And if these four Worthies in their first show thrive, These four will change habits and present the other five . . .
Costard (the Clown presenting the show): O, sir; you have overthrown Alisander the conqueror . . . A conqueror, and afeared to speak! run away for shame, Alisander. [*He retires.*] There an't please you: a foolish, mild man; an honest man, look you, and soon dashed! He is a marvellous good neighbour, faith, and a very good bowler. But for Alisander – alas, you see how 'tis – a little o'erparted [too big a part for him].

Love's Labour's Lost, v.2.

I see the trick on't: here was a consent,
Knowing aforehand of our merriment,
To dash it like a Christmas comedy.

Ibid.

You make faces like mummers.

Coriolanus, ii.1.

And if the boy have not a woman's gift
To rain a shower of commanded tears,
An onion will do well for such a shift.
Which in a napkin being closed conveyed
Shall in despite enforce a watery eye.

The Taming of the Shrew, Induction, 1.

This roaring devil in the old play . . . may pare his nails with a wooden dagger.

Henry V, iv.1.

In a trice, like to the old Vice . . .
Who, with dagger of lath,
In his rage and his wrath,
Cries, Ah, ha! to the Devil.
Like a mad lad
'Pare thy nails, dad,
    Adieu, goodman evil.'

Twelfth Night, iv.2.

[Evidently refers to a regular piece of stage business in old folk-plays –
with which Shakespeare would have been familiar from early days.]

Pat he comes like the catastrophe in the old comedy. My cue is
villainous melancholy.

King Lear, i.2.

He doth it as like one of these harlotry players as ever I see.

1 Henry IV, ii.4.

Are you a comedian?
– No; and yet . . . I swear I am not that I play.

Twelfth Night, i.v.

That sport best pleases that doth least know how:
Where zeal strives to content, and the contents
Die in the zeal of those which it presents;
Their form confounded makes most form in mirth,
When great things labouring perish in their birth.

Love's Labour's Lost, v.2.

Bear it as our Roman actors do,
With untired spirits and formal constancy.

Julius Caesar, ii.1.

I can counterfeit the deep tragedian,
Speak and look back, and pry on every side,
Tremble and start at wagging of a straw;

Intending deep suspicion, ghastly looks
Are at my service, like enforcèd smiles.

                                              Richard III, iii.5.

You have put me now to such a part, which never
I shall discharge to the life.
– Come, come, we'll prompt you.

                                              Coriolanus, iii.2.

Now we speak upon our cue.

                                              Henry V, iii.6.

Is it not monstrous that this player here,
But in a fiction, in a dream of passion,
Could force his soul so to his own conceit
That from her working all his visage wanned –
Tears in his eyes, distraction in his aspect,
A broken voice, and his whole function suiting
With forms to his conceit? And all for nothing!
For Hecuba!
What's Hecuba to him, or he to Hecuba,
That he should weep for her? What would he do
Had he the motive and the cue for passion
That I have? He would drown the stage with tears,
And cleave the general ear with horrid speech,
Make mad the guilty and appal the free,
Confound the ignorant, and amaze indeed
The very faculties of eyes and ears.

                                              Hamlet, ii.2.

Life's but a walking shadow, a poor player
That struts and frets his hour upon the stage
And then is heard no more.

                                              Macbeth, v.5.

The fellow is wise enough to play the Fool,
And to do that well craves a kind of wit.
He must observe their mood on whom he jests,
The quality of persons, and the time,
And, like the haggard, check at every feather
That comes before his eye. This is a practice
As full of labour as a wise man's art.

                                              Twelfth Night, iii.1.

[This combines a reference to the custom in great houses of maintaining a jester to while away the time, with the rôle of the Clown in the theatre. Note too the image from sport, characteristically: there we have William Shakespeare.]

Touring

Weary with toil, I haste me to my bed,
The dear repose for limbs with travel tired;
But then begins a journey in my head
To work my mind, when body's work's expired.
For then my thoughts, from far where I abide,
Intend a zealous pilgrimage to thee.

Sonnet 27

How far I toil, still farther off from thee.

Sonnet 28

How careful was I, when I took my way,
Each trifle under truest bars to thrust,
That to my use it might unused stay
From hands of falsehood, in sure wards of trust.

Sonnet 48

How heavy do I journey on the way
When what I seek, my weary travel's end,
Doth teach that ease and that repose to say
'Thus far the miles are measured from thy friend.'
The beast that bears me, tired with my woe,
Plods dully on, to bear that weight in me,
As if by some instinct the wretch did know
His rider loved not speed, being made from thee:
The bloody spur cannot provoke him on
That sometimes anger thrusts into his hide,
Which heavily he answers with a groan,
More sharp to me than spurring to his side.

For that same groan doth put this in my mind:
My grief lies onward, and my joy behind.

Sonnet 50

Till I return, of posting is no need.
O, what excuse will my poor beast then find,
When swift extremity can seem but slow?
Then should I spur, though mounted on the wind,
In wingèd speed no motion shall I know:
Then can no horse with my desire keep pace.

Sonnet 51

Since I left you mine eye is in my mind,
And that which governs me to go about
Doth part his function and is partly blind.

Sonnet 113

The Young Patron: Southampton

Small show of man was yet upon his chin;
His phoenix-down began but to appear
Like unshorn velvet on that termless skin . . .

His qualities were beauteous as his form,
For maiden-tongued he was and thereof free . . .

That he did in the general bosom reign
Of young, of old, and sexes both enchanted,
To dwell with him in thoughts, or to remain
In personal duty, following where he haunted:
Consents bewitched, ere he desire, have granted;
And dialogued for him what he would say,
Asked their own wills, and made their wills obey.

Many there were that did his picture get,
To serve their eyes, and in it put their mind . . .

So many have, that never touched his hand,
Sweetly supposed them mistress of his heart.

A Lover's Complaint

[This poem was in the Southampton *cache* along with the Sonnets, published by T. Thorp together with them in 1609. So, it was Shakespeare's prentice piece for the youthful patron's patronage, whose personality and characteristics are equally recognisable in this poem of 1591, in *Venus and Adonis*, and the Sonnets of the years following.]

The tender spring upon thy tempting lip
Shows thee unripe, yet mayst thou well be tasted,
Make use of time, let not advantage slip,
Beauty within itself should not be wasted.

Is thine own heart to thine own face affected?
Can thy right hand seize love upon thy left?
Then woo thyself, be of thyself rejected,
Steal thine own freedom, and complain on theft.
Narcissus so himself forsook,
And died to kiss his shadow in the brook.

Upon the earth's increase why shouldst thou feed,
Unless the earth with thy increase be fed?
By law of nature thou art bound to breed,
That thine may live when thou thyself art dead;
And so in spite of death thou dost survive,
In that thy likeness still is left alive.

Venus and Adonis

Thou that art now the world's fresh ornament
And only herald to the gaudy spring.

Sonnet 1

[Henry Wriothesley, pronounced Risley, to become third Earl of Southampton, was born 6 October 1573. Now approaching the end of his minority in his eighteenth year, his family were anxious to see him married, to safeguard the family of which he was the head.]

Look in thy glass and tell the face thou viewest
Now is the time that face should form another . . .
Thou art thy mother's glass and she in thee
Calls back the lovely April of her prime.

Sonnet 3

[Southampton's mother was Mary Browne, daughter of Viscount Montagu.]

So thou, thyself out-going in thy noon,
Unlooked-on diest, unless thou get a son.

Sonnet 7

Make thee another self, for love of me.

Sonnet 10

   dear my love, you know
You had a father: let your son say so.

Sonnet 13

[Southampton's father had died 4 October 1581.]

Now stand you on the top of happy hours,
And many maiden gardens, yet unset,
With virtuous wish would bear your living flowers,
Much liker than your painted counterfeit.

Sonnet 16

But were some child of yours alive that time,
You should live twice, in it and in my rhyme.

Sonnet 17

Shall I compare thee to a summer's day?
Thou art more lovely and more temperate.

Sonnet 18

A woman's face with Nature's own hand painted
Hast thou, the master-mistress of my passion;
A woman's gentle heart, but not acquainted
With shifting change, as is false women's fashion;
An eye more bright than theirs, less false in rolling . . .
A man in hue, all hues in his controlling,
Which steals men's eyes and women's souls amazeth.
And for a woman wert thou first created,
Till Nature, as she wrought thee, fell a-doting,
And by addition me of thee defeated,
By adding one thing to my purpose nothing.
But since she pricked thee out for women's pleasure,
Mine be thy love, and thy love's use their treasure.

Sonnet 20

[This utterly candid Sonnet makes perfectly clear that Shakespeare had
no interest in the ambivalent youth sexually: his love for him was entirely
platonic. And nearly ten years older, he felt a quasi-parental responsi-
bility for the youth who was fatherless, now coming out into the
temptations of the world.]

Lord of my love, to whom in vassalage
Thy merit hath my duty strongly knit,
To thee I send this written ambassage
To witness duty, not to show my wit:
Duty so great, which wit so poor as mine
May make seem bare, in wanting words to show it,

1.   William Shakespeare

2a. Southampton at the time of the Sonnets

2b. Ralegh at the time of his fall

3. Elizabeth I at the time of the Kenilworth Entertainments

4.   King James I

5.   Essex in the 1590's

y Carey
d Hunsdon

ʀ ᴋ Gᴇʀᴀʀᴅꜱ.

Æᴛᴀᴛɪꜱ ꜱᴠ
ᴀɴ° 159

6.   Lord Chamberlain Hunsdon, Patron of Shakespeare's Company

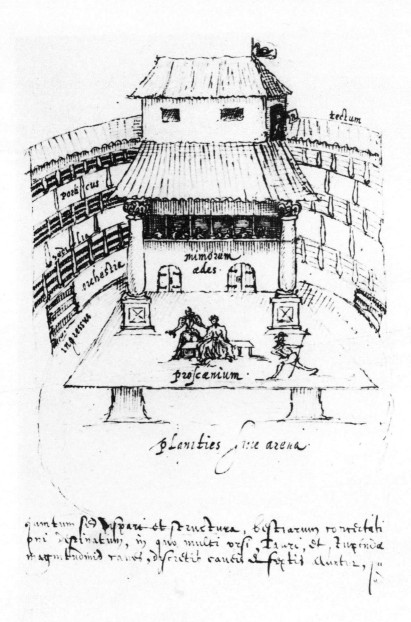

7. An Elizabethan theatre

8. Where Shakespeare was baptised and buried

But that I hope some good conceit of thine
In thy soul's thought, all naked, will bestow it.

Sonnet 26

['Duty' is thrice emphasised, for the Sonnets are written in the course of
duty to the patron.]

Venus and Adonis

'*Vilia miretur vulgus; mihi flavus Apollo
Pocula Castalia plena ministret aqua.*'

[Let the mob admire base things: but to me let Apollo minister water
from purest springs.]

To the Right Honourable Henry Wriothesley, Earl of Southampton
and Baron of Titchfield.
Right Honourable, I know not how I shall offend in dedicating my
unpolished lines to your lordship, nor how the world will censure
me for choosing so strong a prop to support so weak a burden. Only,
if your honour seem but pleased, I account myself highly praised,
and vow to take advantage of all idle hours, till I have honoured you
with some graver labour. But if the first heir of my invention prove
deformed, I shall be sorry it had so noble a godfather, and never
after ear[1] so barren a land, for fear it yield me still [ever] so bad a
harvest. I leave it to your honourable survey, and your honour to
your heart's content; which I wish may always answer your own
wish and the world's hopeful expectation.

Your honour's in all duty,
William Shakespeare.

Venus and Adonis, Dedication

Why didst thou promise such a beauteous day
And make me travel forth without my cloak,
To let base clouds o'ertake me in my way? . . .
'Tis not enough that through the cloud thou break,
To dry the rain on my storm-beaten face,
For no man well of such a salve can speak
That heals the wound and cures not the disgrace.
Nor can thy shame give physic to my grief –
Though thou repent yet I have still the loss:

---

[1] A countryman's word, meaning to plough.

The offender's sorrow lends but weak relief
To him that bears the strong offence's cross.

Sonnet 34

No more be grieved at that which thou hast done:
Roses have thorns, and silver fountains mud,
Clouds and eclipses stain both moon and sun,
And loathsome canker lives in sweetest bud.
All men make faults, and even I in this,
Authorising thy trespass with compare,
Myself corrupting, salving thy amiss,
Excusing thy sins more than thy sins are . . .
Such civil war is in my love and hate
That I an accessory needs must be
To that sweet thief which sourly robs from me.

Sonnet 35

[These two sonnets have precisely parallel passages in *The Two Gentlemen
of Verona*, Act i, Scenes 1 and 3. The theme of the play is that of the
friendship between two men in conflict for the same woman. At the end
one of them gives up his mistress to the other – precisely what happens in
the Sonnets. The play's inspiration is autobiographical, the date
1592–3.]

Let me confess that we two must be twain,
Although our undivided loves are one:
So shall those blots that do with me remain,
Without thy help, by me be borne alone.
In our two loves there is but one respect,
Though in our lives a separable spite,
Which though it alters not love's sole effect,
Yet doth it steal sweet hours from love's delight.
I may not evermore acknowledge thee,
Lest my bewailèd guilt should do thee shame,
Nor thou with public kindness honour me,
Unless thou take that honour from thy name.

Sonnet 36

Take all my loves, my love, yea, take them all:
What hast thou then more than thou hadst before? . . .
I do forgive thy robbery, gentle thief,
Although thou steal thee all my poverty.

Sonnet 40

That thou hast her, it is not all my grief,
And yet it may be said I loved her dearly;
That she hath thee is of my wailing chief –
A loss in love that touches me more nearly . . .
Both find each other, and I lose both twain,
And both for my sake lay on me this cross.

Sonnet 42

Against that time, if ever that time come,
When I shall see thee frown on my defects,
Whenas thy love hath cast his utmost sum . . .
Against that time when thou shalt strangely pass,
And scarcely greet me with that sun, thine eye,
When love converted from the thing it was,
Shall reasons find of settled gravity.

Sonnet 49

What is your substance, whereof are you made?
Describe Adonis, and the counterfeit
Is poorly imitated after you.

Sonnet 53

[*Venus and Adonis* was published by Shakespeare's fellow townsman from
Stratford, Richard Field, in 1593. The poem was being written
contemporaneously with these Sonnets.]

Being your slave, what should I do but tend
Upon the hours and times of your desire?
I have no precious time at all to spend,
Nor services to do, till you require.
Nor dare I chide the world-without-end hour
Whilst I, my sovereign, watch the clock for you,
Nor think the bitterness of absence sour
When you have bid your servant once adieu.
Nor dare I question with my jealous thought
Where you may be, or your affairs suppose,
But like a sad slave stay and think of naught
Save, where you are, how happy you make those.

Sonnet 57

That God forbid, that made me first your slave,
I should in thought control your times of pleasure,
Or at your hand the account of hours to crave,
Being your vassal, bound to stay your leisure.
O, let me suffer, being at your beck,
The imprisoned absence of your liberty,
And patience tame to sufferance, bide each check,
Without accusing you of injury . . .
I am to wait, though waiting so be hell,
Not blame your pleasure, be it ill or well.

Sonnet 58

[These two sonnets reveal the rather humiliating side to being dependent on a patron.]

Is it thy spirit that thou send'st from thee
So far from home into my deeds to pry,
To find out shames and idle hours in me,
The scope and tenure of thy jealousy?

Sonnet 61

So are you to my thoughts as food to life,
Or as sweet-seasoned showers are to the ground . . .
Now proud as an enjoyer, and anon
Doubting the filching age will steal his treasure;
Now counting best to be with you alone,
Then bettered that the world may see my pleasure;
Sometimes all full with feasting on your sight,
And by and by clean starvèd for a look:
Possessing or pursuing no delight,
Save what is had or must from you be took.

Sonnet 75

Farewell! thou art too dear for my possessing –
And like enough thou know'st thy estimate . . .
Thyself thou gav'st, thy own worth then not knowing,
Or me, to whom thou gav'st it, else mistaking.
So thy great gift, upon misprision growing,
Comes home again, on better judgment making.

Sonnet 87

When thou shalt be disposed to set me light
And place my merit in the eye of scorn,
Upon thy side against myself I'll fight . . .
With mine own weakness being best acquainted,
Upon thy part I can set down a story
Of faults concealed, wherein I am attainted.

Sonnet 88

So shall I live, supposing thou art true,
Like a deceivèd husband; so love's face
May still seem love to me, though altered new:
Thy looks with me, thy heart in other place.

Sonnet 93

How sweet and lovely dost thou make the shame
Which, like a canker in the fragrant rose,
Doth spot the beauty of thy budding name!
O, in what sweets dost thou thy sins enclose!
That tongue that tells the story of thy days,
Making lascivious comments on thy sport,
Cannot dispraise but in a kind of praise:
Naming thy name blesses an ill report.

Sonnet 95

Some say thy fault is youth, some wantonness,
Some say thy grace is youth and gentle sport;
Both grace and faults are loved of more and less:
Thou mak'st faults graces that to thee resort.

Sonnet 96

To me, fair friend, you never can be old,
For as you were when first your eye I eyed,
Such seems your beauty still: three winters cold
Have from the forests shook three summers' pride,
Three beauteous springs to yellow autumn turned
In process of the seasons have I seen,
Three April perfumes in three hot Junes burned,
Since first I saw you fresh, which yet are green.

Sonnet 104

[These dates are the winters of 1591–2, 1592–3, 1593–4, with their
following seasons.]

The Rape of Lucrece

To the Right Honourable Henry Wriothesley, Earl of Southampton and Baron of Titchfield. The love I dedicate to your lordship is without end; whereof this pamphlet, without beginning, is but a superfluous moiety. The warrant I have of your honourable disposition, not the worth of my untutored lines, makes it assured of acceptance. What I have done is yours; what I have to do is yours; being part in all I have, devoted yours. Were my worth greater, my duty would show greater; meantime, as it is, it is bound to your lordship, to whom I wish long life, still lengthened with happiness.
Your lordship's in all duty,
William Shakespeare.

[Elizabethans used the word love, as we sometimes do, to mean friendship as well as erotic, sexual love. But Shakespeare would never have publicly proclaimed his love for the young patron, if it had been homosexual love. Very imperceptive of people not to see that. Duty is yet again recognised; most important is the asseveration of Shakespeare's devotion to one to whom he owed an incomparable debt, above all – for a writer – inspiration:

Since all alike my songs and praises be
To one, of one, still such, and ever so.]

The Dark Lady:
Emilia Lanier

ఠ

O, if in black my lady's brows be decked
It mourns that painting and usurping hair
Should ravish doters with a false aspect;
And therefore is she born to make black fair.
Her favour turns the fashion of the days,
For native blood is counted painting now;
And therefore red, that would avoid dispraise,
Paints itself black to imitate her brow.

Love's Labour's Lost, IV.3.

[In this play, a skit on the Southampton circle, Shakespeare depicts himself as Berowne, his dark young mistress as Rosaline.]

Therefore my mistress' eyes are raven black,
Her eyes so suited, and they mourners seem
As such who, not born fair, no beauty lack.

Sonnet 127

How oft when thou, my music, music play'st
Upon that blessèd wood whose motion sounds
With thy sweet fingers, when thou gently sway'st
The wiry concord that mine ear confounds,
Do I envy those jacks that nimble leap
To kiss the tender inward of thy hand;
Whilst my poor lips, which should that harvest reap,
At the wood's boldness by thee blushing stand.
To be so tickled they would change their state
And situation with those dancing chips,
O'er whom thy fingers walk with gentle gait,
Making dead wood more blest than living lips.

Since saucy jacks so happy are in this,
Give them thy fingers, me thy lips to kiss.

Sonnet 128

I grant I never saw a goddess go [walk]:
My mistress, when she walks, treads on the ground.
And yet, by heaven, I think my love as rare
As any she belied by false compare.

Sonnet 130

Thou art as tyrannous, so as thou art,
As those whose beauties proudly make them cruel;
For well thou know'st to my dear doting heart
Thou art the fairest and most precious jewel.
Yet, in good faith, some say that thee behold
Thy face hath not the power to make love groan . . .
Thy black is fairest in my judgment's place:
In nothing art thou black save in thy deeds,
And thence this slander, as I think, proceeds.

Sonnet 131

Thine eyes I love, and they, as pitying me,
Knowing thy heart torments me with disdain,
Have put on black, and loving mourners be . . .
O let it then as well beseem thy heart
To mourn for me, since mourning doth thee grace,
And suit thy pity like in every part.

Sonnet 132

Beshrew that heart that makes my heart to groan
For that deep wound it gives my friend and me!
Is't not enough to torture me alone
But slave to slavery my sweet'st friend must be?
Me from myself thy cruel eye hath taken,
And my next self thou harder hast engrossed:
Of him, myself, and thee I am forsaken,
A torment thrice threefold thus to be crossed.

Sonnet 133

So, now I have confessed that he is thine
And I myself am mortgaged to thy will . . .

But thou wilt not, nor he will not be free,
For thou art covetous and he is kind;
He learned but surety-like to write for me,
Under that bond that him as fast doth bind . . .
Thou usurer that put'st forth all to use,
And sue a friend 'came debtor for my sake . . .
Him have I lost; thou hast both him and me;
He pays the whole, and yet am I not free.

Sonnet 134

Whoever hath her wish, thou hast thy will,
And will to boot, and Will in overplus:[1]
More than enough am I that vex thee still [ever],
To thy sweet will making addition thus.
Wilt thou, whose will is large and spacious,
Not once vouchsafe to hide my will in thine?
Shall will in others seem right gracious
And in my will no fair acceptance shine? . . .
So thou, being rich in will, add to thy will
One will of mine, to make thy large will more.

Sonnet 135

If thy soul check thee that I come so near,
Swear to thy blind soul that I was thy will,
And will thy soul knows is admitted there;
Thus far, for love, my love-suit, sweet, fulfil.
Will will fulfil the treasure of thy love –
Ay, fill it full with wills, and my will one.
In things of great receipt with ease we prove
Among a number one is reckoned none.
Then in the number let me pass untold,
Though in thy store's account I one must be . . .
Make but my name thy love, and love that still,
And then thou lovest me, for my name is Will.

Sonnet 136

Thou blind fool, love, what dost thou to mine eyes
That they behold, and see not what they see? . . .

---

[1] i.e. she has her own sex, her husband's 'to boot' (as well) and Will
Shakespeare's 'in overplus'.

If eyes, corrupt by over-partial looks,
Be anchored in the bay where all men ride . . .
Why should my eyes think that a several plot
Which my heart knows the wide world's common place?

Sonnet 137

When my love swears that she is made of truth
I do believe her, though I know she lies,
That she might think me some untutored youth,
Unlearnèd in the world's false subtleties.
Thus vainly thinking that she thinks me young,
Although she knows my days are past the best . . .
O, love's best habit is in seeming trust,
And age in love loves not to have years told.
Therefore I lie with her and she with me,
And in our faults by lies we flattered be.

Sonnet 138

Tell me thou lov'st elsewhere, but in my sight,
Dear heart, forbear to glance thine eye aside.

Sonnet 139

If I might teach thee wit, better it were
Though not to love, yet, love, to tell me so . . .
Mad slanderers by mad ears believèd be.
That I may not be so, nor thou belied,
Bear thine eyes straight though thy proud heart go wide.

Sonnet 140

In faith, I do not love thee with mine eyes,
For they in thee a thousand errors note,
But 'tis my heart that loves what they despise . . .
But my five wits, nor my five senses can
Dissuade one foolish heart from serving thee . . .
Thy proud heart's slave and vassal wretch to be:
Only my plague thus far I count my gain
That she that makes me sin awards me pain.

Sonnet 141

Love is my sin, and thy dear virtue hate,
Hate of my sin, grounded on sinful loving.

O, but with mine compare thou thine own state
And thou shalt find it merits not reproving.
Or, if it do, not from those lips of thine
That have profaned their scarlet ornaments
And sealed false bonds of love as oft as mine,
Robbed others' beds' revènues of their rents.
Be it lawful I love thee, as thou lov'st those
Whom thine eyes woo as mine importune thee.

                                    Sonnet 142

So runn'st thou after that which flies from thee,
Whilst I, thy babe, chase thee afar behind;
But if thou catch thy hope, turn back to me
And play the mother's part, kiss me, be kind.

                                    Sonnet 143

Two loves I have, of comfort and despair,
Which like two spirits do suggest me still:
The better angel is a man right fair,
The worser spirit a woman coloured ill.
To win me soon to hell, my female evil
Tempteth my better angel from my side,
And would corrupt my saint to be a devil,
Wooing his purity with her foul pride.
And whether that my angel be turned fiend
Suspect I may, yet not directly tell;
But being both from me, both to each friend,
I guess one angel in another's hell.
Yet this shall I ne'er know, but live in doubt,
Till my bad angel fire my good one out.

                                    Sonnet 144

My love is as a fever, longing still [ever]
For that which longer nurseth the disease;
Feeding on that which doth preserve the ill,
The uncertain sickly appetite to please.
My reason, the physician to my love,
Angry that his prescriptions are not kept . . .
Past cure I am, now reason is past care,
And frantic-mad with evermore unrest . . .

For I have sworn thee fair, and thought thee bright,
Who art as black as hell, as dark as night.

Sonnet 147

O me! what eyes hath love put in my head,
Which have no correspondence with true sight;
Or, if they have, where is my judgement fled
That censures [judges] falsely what they see aright?
If that be fair whereon my false eyes dote,
What means the world to say it is not so?
O cunning love, with tears thou keep'st me blind,
Lest eyes well-seeing thy foul faults should find.

Sonnet 148

Canst thou, O cruel, say I love thee not,
When I against myself with thee partake? . . .
Who hateth thee that I do call my friend;
On whom frown'st thou that I do fawn upon? . . .
When all my best doth worship thy defect,
Commanded by the motion of thine eyes.

Sonnet 149

O from what power hast thou this powerful might
With insufficiency my heart to sway,
To make me give the lie to my true sight? . . .
Whence hast thou this becoming of things ill,
That in the very refuse of thy deeds
There is such strength and warrantise of skill
That, in my mind, thy worst all best exceeds?
Who taught thee how to make me love thee more,
The more I hear and see just cause of hate?
O, though I love what others do abhor,
With others thou shouldst not abhor my state.
If thy unworthiness raised love in me,
More worthy I to be beloved of thee.

Sonnet 150

O, 'tis the curse in love and still approved [proved]
When women cannot love where they're beloved.

The Two Gentlemen of Verona, v.4.

My soul doth tell my body that he may
Triumph in love: flesh stays no farther reason,
But rising at thy name doth point out thee
As his triumphant prize. Proud of this pride,
He is contented thy poor drudge to be,
To stand in thy affairs, fall by thy side.
No want of conscience hold it that I call
Her 'love', for whose dear love I rise and fall.

Sonnet 151

In loving thee thou know'st I am forsworn,
But thou art twice forsworn, to me love swearing:
In act thy bed-vow broke and new faith torn,
In vowing new hate after new love bearing.
But why of two oaths' breach do I accuse thee,
When I break twenty? I am perjured most,
For all my vows are oaths but to misuse thee,
And all my honest faith in thee is lost.

Sonnet 152

I, sick withal, the help of bath desired
And thither hied, a sad distempered guest.

Sonnet 153

Love's Labour's Lost reflects the earlier, happier stage of Shakespeare's affair with his dark lady, Rosaline. Katharine describes her as 'light', and

of such a merry, nimble, stirring spirit.

Rosaline: What's your dark meaning, mouse, of this light word?
Katharine: A light condition in a beauty dark.
Rosaline: Look what you do, you do it still [ever] in the dark.
Katharine: So do not you, for you're a light wench.

This is amply borne out by the Sonnets.
   Rosaline promises to torment Berowne:

How I would make him fawn, and beg, and seek,
And wait the season, and observe the times,
And spend his prodigal wits in bootless rhymes,

And shape his service wholly to my hests,
And make him proud to make me proud that jests!
So planet-like would I o'er-sway his state,
That he should be my fool, and I his fate.

This was precisely how Emilia behaved in fact. Shakespeare, completely aware, as in the Sonnets, makes Katharine comment:

None are so surely caught, when they are catched,
As wit turned fool.

We see in the Sonnets, as well as from what Robert Greene said of him, his confidence in his own 'wit', i.e. intelligence. Here he refers to his 'prodigal wits', as in his reference to himself in *The Two Gentlemen* he assures us that 'eating love inhabits in the finest wits of all'.

We may well see a later reflection of this experience – especially of Sonnets 137 and 141 – on the theme of eyes' betrayal – in Cressida's faithlessness:

Ah, poor our sex, this fault in us I find,
The error of our eye directs our mind.
What error leads must err. O then conclude,
Minds swayed by eyes are full of turpitude.

And Troilus':

Shall I not lie in publishing a truth,
Sith yet there is a credence in my heart,
An esperance so obstinately strong,
That doth invert the attest of eyes and ears.

Troilus and Cressida, v.2.

Love

ॐ

Friendship is constant in all other things
Save in the office and affairs of love:
Therefore all hearts in love use their own tongues,
Let every eye negotiate for itself
And trust no agent.

Much Ado About Nothing, II.1.

But love, first learnèd in a lady's eyes,
Lives not alone immurèd in the brain,
But with the motion of all elements,
Courses as swift as thought in every power,
And gives to every power a double power,
Above their functions and their offices . . .
Love's feeling is more soft and sensible
Than are the tender horns of cockled snails;
Love's tongue proves dainty Bacchus gross in taste . . .
Never durst poet touch a pen to write
Until his ink were tempered with love's sighs;
O, then his lips would ravish savage ears . . .

Love's Labour's Lost, IV.3.

How old art thou?
– Not so young, sir, to love a woman for singing.

King Lear, I.4.

[Remember Emilia Lanier's musicality.]

O spirit of love! how quick and fresh art thou,
That, notwithstanding thy capacity

87

Receiveth as the sea, nought enters there –
Of what validity and pitch soe'er –
But falls into abatement and low price,
Even in a minute.

Twelfth Night, i.1.

O, mistress mine, where are you roaming?
O, stay and hear, your true love's coming,
　　　That can sing both high and low.
Trip no further, pretty sweeting;
Journeys end in lovers meeting,
　　　Every wise man's son doth know.

What is love? 'Tis not hereafter:
Present mirth hath present laughter,
　　　What's to come is still unsure.
In delay there lies no plenty;
Then come kiss me, sweet and twenty,
　　　Youth's a stuff will not endure.

Twelfth Night, ii.3.

For such as I am all true lovers are:
Unstaid and skittish in all motions else
Save in the constant image of the creature
That is beloved.

Twelfth Night, ii.4.

How silver-sweet sound lovers' tongues by night,
Like softest music to attending ears!

Romeo and Juliet, ii.2.

Alas that love, so gentle in his view,
Should be so tyrannous and rough in proof!

Romeo and Juliet, i.1.

If thou rememberest not the slightest folly
That ever love did make thee run into
Thou hast not loved.

As You Like It, ii.4.

Lovers can see to do their amorous rites
By their own beauties; or, if love be blind,
It best agrees with night.

Romeo and Juliet, iii.2.

If she'd do the deed of darkness.

Pericles, iv.6.

A serving-man, proud in mind and heart that served the lust of my
mistress's heart and did the deed of darkness with her.

King Lear, iii.4.

This is the monstruosity in love – that the will is infinite and the
execution confined, that the desire is boundless and the act a slave
to limit.

Troilus and Cressida, iii.2.

To be wise, and love,
Exceeds man's might: that dwells with gods above.

Troilus and Cressida, iii.2.

Though Love use Reason for his physician, he admits him not for
his counsellor.

The Merry Wives of Windsor, ii.1.

Love is not love
When it is mingled with regards [considerations] that stand
Aloof from the main point.

King Lear, i.1.

Prosperity's the very bond of love,
Whose fresh complexion and whose heart together,
Affliction alters.

The Winter's Tale, iv.3.

There is no woman's sides
Can bide the beating of so strong a passion
As love doth give my heart: no woman's heart
So big to hold so much: they lack retention.
Alas, their love may be called appetite,

No motion of the liver, but the palate,
That suffer surfeit, cloyment, and revolt.

Twelfth Night, ii.4.

When love begins to sicken and decay
It useth an enforcèd ceremony.

Julius Caesar, iv.2.

In love
Who respects friend?

The Two Gentlemen of Verona, v.4.

The Rival Poet:
Christopher Marlowe

So oft have I invoked thee for my muse . . .
As every alien pen hath got my use
And under thee their poesy disperse.
Thine eyes, that taught the dumb on high to sing . . .
Have added feathers to the learned's wing
And given grace a double majesty.

Sonnet 78

[Shakespeare speaks several times respectfully, if not deferentially, of the
'learned', i.e. university-educated.]

But now my gracious numbers are decayed
And my sick muse doth give another place.
I grant, sweet love, thy lovely argument
Deserves the travail of a worthier pen.
Yet what of thee thy poet doth invent
He robs thee of, and pays it thee again.

Sonnet 79

O, how I faint when I of you do write,
Knowing a better spirit doth use your name . . .
But since your worth, wide as the ocean is,
The humble as the proudest sail doth bear,
My saucy bark, inferior far to his,
On your broad main doth wilfully appear.
Your shallowest help will hold me up afloat,
Whilst he upon your soundless deep doth ride:
Or, being wrecked, I am a worthless boat,
He of tall building and of goodly pride.

Then if he thrive and I be cast away,
The worst was this: my love was my decay.

Sonnet 80

[Shakespeare courteously accepted the fact of Marlowe's superiority as a
writer to date.]

I grant thou wert not married to my muse . . .
And therefore art enforced to seek anew
Some fresher stamp of the time-bettering days.
And do so, love: yet when they have devised
What strainèd touches rhetoric can lend,
Thou, truly fair, wert truly sympathised
In true plain words by thy true-telling friend.

Sonnet 82

This silence for my sin you did impute,
Which shall be most my glory, being dumb;
For I impair not beauty, being mute
When others would give life and bring a tomb.
There lives more life in one of your fair eyes
Than both your poets can in praise devise.

Sonnet 83

My tongue-tied Muse in manners holds her still,
While comments of your praise, richly compiled,
Reserve their character with golden quill
And precious phrase by all the Muses filed.
I think good thoughts, whilst other write good words,
And like unlettered clerk still [ever] cry 'Amen'
To every hymn that able spirit affords
In polished form of well-refinèd pen.

Sonnet 85

[A further recognition of Marlowe's superior artistry, borne out by his
Hero and Leander.]

Was it the proud full sail of his great verse,
Bound for the prize of all-too-precious you,
That did my ripe thoughts in my brain inhearse . . .
Was it his spirit, by spirits taught to write

Above a mortal pitch, that struck me dead?
No, neither he, nor his compeers by night
Giving him aid, my verse astonishèd.
He, nor that affable familiar ghost
Which nightly gulls him with intelligence,
As victors of my silence cannot boast:
I was not sick of any fear from thence –
But when your countenance filled up his line,
Then lacked I matter: that enfeebled mine.

Sonnet 86

[Marlowe's 'mighty line' – Jonson's phrase for it – was recognised by all: his contribution of splendid poetry to the theatre. His imagery shows him as a night-writer, while he knew about trafficking with the spirits. Mephistopheles gulled Dr Faustus nightly with knowledge in Marlowe's most famous play.]

Upon some book I love I'll pray for thee.
– That's on some shallow story of deep love,
How young Leander crossed the Hellespont.

The Two Gentlemen of Verona, I.1.

Leander, he would have lived many a fair year, though Hero had turned nun, if it had not been for a hot midsummer night. For, good youth, he went but forth to wash him in the Hellespont and, being taken with the cramp, was drowned.

As You Like It, IV.1.

[The publication of Marlowe's *Hero and Leander* in 1598 revived these memories; the play is of that year.]

. . . It strikes a man more dead than a great reckoning in a little room.

As You Like It, III.3.

[Shakespeare knew well how Marlowe came by his end in the little Deptford tavern; the inquest recorded the quarrel over 'le reckoning'.]

Dead shepherd, now I find thy saw of might:
'Who ever loved that loved not at first sight?'

As You Like It, III.5.

[In 1592, when Shakespeare was writing this play, Marlowe was writing his *Hero and Leander* for Southampton's patronage in rivalry with Shakespeare's *Venus and Adonis*. Hence too the following reference in the same play at the same time. Southampton's two poets were familiar with each other's work.]

> A ladder
> Would serve to scale another Hero's tower,
> So bold Leander would adventure it.
>
> *The Two Gentlemen of Verona*, III.1.

> How now, Mephistophilus!
>
> *The Merry Wives of Windsor*, I.1.

[Marlowe's *Dr Faustus* was perhaps the most popular of all Elizabethan plays – not surprising that Shakespeare refers to it. This was the spirit that gulled Faustus at night with forbidden knowledge – intelligence.]

> Set spurs and away, like three German devils, three Doctor Faustuses.
>
> *The Merry Wives of Windsor*, IV.5.

> To shallow rivers to whose falls
> Melodious pirds sing madrigals;
> There will we make our peds of roses,
> And a thousand fragrant posies.
>
> *The Merry Wives of Windsor*, III.1.

[Here Shakespeare is making fun of Marlowe's most popular poem, 'Come live with me and be my love', by making a Welsh curate sing it with Welsh accent.]

> How sweet a thing it is to wear a crown,
> Within whose circuit is Elysium
> And all that poets feign of bliss and joy.
>
> *3 Henry* VI, I.2.

[The poet here is Marlowe, whose lines in *Tamburlane* Shakespeare is here echoing. At this early time they were writing for, their plays produced by, the same companies.]

Come unto these yellow sands,
    And then take hands;
Curtsied when you have, and kissed –
    The wild waves whist.

The Tempest, I.2.

['The wild waves whist' is Marlowe's phrase from years before – which had remained in Shakespeare's marvellous actor's-memory. It is touching that in this, his next-to-the-last play, he should be remembering the poet of genius who had perished so casually many years before: the greatest influence upon, and inspiration for, his own work, though so different a man, their natures in such contrast.]

On Poetry

ﾉ

The poet's eye, in a fine frenzy rolling,
Doth glance from heaven to earth, from earth to heaven;
And as imagination bodies forth
The forms of things unknown, the poet's pen
Turns them to shapes, and gives to airy nothing
A local habitation and a name.
Such tricks hath strong imagination . . .

A Midsummer Night's Dream, v.1.

Leander, the good swimmer, Troilus, the first employer of
panders, and a whole bookful of these quondam carpet-mongers,
whose names yet run smoothly in the even road of a blank verse . . .
I cannot show it in rhyme . . . I can find out no rhyme to 'lady' but
'baby', an innocent rhyme; for 'scorn', 'horn', a hard rhyme; for
'school', 'fool', a babbling rhyme. Very ominous endings.

Much Ado About Nothing, v.2.

As Horace says in his – what, my soul, verses?

Love's Labour's Lost, iv.2.

Never durst poet touch a pen to write
Until his ink were tempered with Love's sighs.
O, then his lines would ravish savage ears,
And plant in tyrants mild humility.

Love's Labour's Lost, iv.2.

[Written at the height of his affair with the Dark Lady, who appears in
the play as Rosaline, himself as Berowne. His lines did not, however,
reduce his tyrant – 'tyrannous' was his word for her – to humility.]

96

Much is the force of heaven-bred poesy . . .
You must lay lime to tangle her desires
By wailful sonnets, whose composèd rhymes
Should be full-fraught with serviceable vows.
Say that upon the altar of her beauty
You sacrifice your tears, your sighs, your heart.
Write till your ink be dry, and with your tears
Moist it again, and frame some feeling line
That may discover such integrity.
For Orpheus' lute was strung with poets' sinews,
Whose golden touch could soften steel and stones,
Make tigers tame and huge leviathans
Forsake unsounded deeps to dance on sands.

The Two Gentlemen of Verona, iii.2.

Truly, I would the gods had made thee poetical.
– I do not know what 'poetical' is. Is it honest in deed and word. Is it
a true thing?
No, truly, for the truest poetry is the most feigning. And lovers are
given to poetry. And what they swear in poetry may be said as lovers
they do feign.

As You Like It, iii.3.

You find not the apostrophes, and so miss the accent. Let me
supervise the canzonet. Here are only numbers ratified; but for the
elegance, facility, and golden cadence of poesy, *caret* [it is wanting].
Ovidius Naso was the man; and why indeed *Naso*, but for smelling
out the odoriferous flowers of fancy, the jerks of invention? *Imitari* is
nothing; so doth the hound his master, the ape his keeper, the
attired horse his rider.

Love's Labour's Lost, iv.2.

The lady shall say her mind freely, or the blank verse shall halt for it.

Hamlet, ii.2.

Did you hear these verses?
– Some of them had in them more feet than the verses would bear.
That's no matter, the feet might bear the verses.
– Ay, but the feet were lame and could not bear themselves without
the verse, and therefore stood lamely in the verse.

As You Like It, iii.2.

God be with you, if you talk in blank verse.

As You Like It, iv.1.

On his own Poetry

Why is my verse so barren of new pride,
So far from variation or quick change?
Why with the time do I not glance aside
To new-found methods and to compounds strange?[1]
Why write I still all one, ever the same,
And keep invention in a noted weed,
That every word doth almost tell my name,
Showing their birth and where they did proceed?
O, know, sweet love, I always write of you,
And you and love are still [ever] my argument.

Sonnet 76

So oft have I invoked thee for my muse,
And found such fair assistance in my verse,
As every alien pen hath got my use
And under thee their poesy disperse.

Sonnet 78

Your monument shall be my gentle verse,
Which eyes not yet created shall o'er read;
And tongues-to-be your being shall rehearse,
When all the breathers of this world are dead:
You still [ever] shall live – such virtue hath my pen –
Where breath most breathes, even in the mouths of men.

Sonnet 81

Where art thou, Muse, that thou forget'st so long
To speak of that which gives thee all thy might?

[1] e.g. the strained, less easy, poetry of Chapman or Donne.

Spend'st thou thy fury on some worthless song,
Darkening thy power to lend base subjects light?
Return, forgetful Muse, and straight redeem
In gentle numbers time so idly spent;
Sing to the ear that doth thy lays esteem
And gives thy pen both skill and argument.

Sonnet 100

Then do thy office, Muse: I teach thee how
To make him seem long hence as he shows now.

Sonnet 101

Alack, what poverty my Muse brings forth,
That having such a scope to show her pride
The argument, all bare, is of more worth
Than when it hath my added praise beside.
O, blame me not, if I no more can write!
Look in your glass and there appears a face
That overgoes my blunt invention quite,
Dulling my lines and doing me disgrace.

Sonnet 103

. . . all alike my songs and praises be
To one, of one, still [ever] such, and ever so . . .
Therefore my verse to constancy confined,
One thing expressing, leaves out difference.

Sonnet 105

I once wrote a sonnet in his praise, and began thus: 'Wonder of
nature.'
– I have heard a sonnet begin so to one's mistress.

Henry V, III.7.

Our poesy is as a gum which oozes
From whence 'tis nourished . . .[1]
                    Our gentle flame
Provokes itself, and like the current flies
Each bound it chafes.

Timon of Athens, I.1.

---

[1] i.e. his own poetry flowed naturally and spontaneously. Heming and Condell
said that he 'never blotted a line', Ben Jonson grumpily 'would he had blotted a
thousand'. Everything about William Shakespeare coheres and makes him clear.

Countryman and Country Lore

Either I mistake your shape and making quite,
Or else you are that shrewd and knavish sprite
Called Robin Goodfellow. Are you not he
That frights the maidens of the villagery;
Skim milk, and sometime labour in the quern,
And bootless make the breathless housewife churn;
And sometime make the drink to bear no barm,
Mislead night-wanderers, laughing at their harm?
Those that Hobgoblin call you and sweet Puck,
You do their work, and they shall have good luck.

A Midsummer Night's Dream, II.1.

Queen Mab! What's she?
– She is the fairies' midwife, and she comes
In shape no bigger than an agate stone
On the forefinger of an alderman,[1]
Drawn with a team of little atomies
Athwart men's noses as they lie asleep . . .
        This is that very Mab
That plats the manes of horses in the night,
And bakes the elf-locks in foul sluttish hairs,
Which once untangled much misfortune bodes.

Romeo and Juliet, I.4.

Night's swift dragons cut the clouds full fast,
And yonder shines Aurora's harbinger,
At whose approach ghosts, wandering here and there,

[1] Remember that Shakespeare's father was an alderman.

Troop home to churchyards: damnèd spirits all
That in crossways and floods have burial,
Already to their wormy beds are gone.

A Midsummer Night's Dream, iii.2.

Now it is the time of night
   That the graves, all gaping wide,
Every one lets forth his sprite,
   In the churchway paths to glide . . .
Through the house give glimmering light
   By the dead and drowsy fire
Every elf and fairy sprite
   Hop as light as bird from briar . . .

Now until the break of day,
Through this house each fairy stray.
To the best bride-bed will we,
Which by us shall blessèd be;
And the issue there create
Ever shall be fortunate.

A Midsummer Night's Dream, v.2.

Ye elves of hills, brooks, standing lakes, and groves;
And ye that on the sands with printless foot
Do chase the ebbing Neptune and do fly him
When he comes back; you demi-puppets that
By moonshine do the green sour ringlets make
Whereof the ewe not bites; and you whose pastime
Is to make midnight mushrooms; that rejoice
To hear the solemn curfew.

The Tempest, v.1.

You sun-burnt sicklemen, of August weary,
Come hither from the furrow, and be merry:
Make holiday; your rye-straw hats put on,
And these fresh nymphs encounter every one
In country footing.

The Tempest, iv.1.

Look, the unfolding star calls forth the shepherd.

Measure for Measure, iv.2.

Let me see: every 'leven wether tods – every tod yields pound and odd shilling: fifteen hundred shorn, what comes the wool to? . . . I cannot do it without counters. Let me see: what am I to buy for our sheep-shearing feast? 'Three pound of sugar; five pound of currants, rice.' What will this sister of mine do with rice? But my father hath made her mistress of the feast, and she lays it on. She hath made me four-and-twenty nosegays for the shearers, three-man song-men all, and very good ones. But they are most of them means and bases; but one Puritan among them, and he sings psalms to hornpipes. I must have saffron to colour the warden pies; mace, dates – none, that's out of my note; nutmegs seven; a race or two of ginger – but that I may beg; four pound of prunes, and as many of raisins o' the sun.

The Winter's Tale, iv.2.

Master, there is three carters, three shepherds, three neat-herds, three swine-herds, that have made themselves all men of hair. They call themselves Saltiers; and they have a dance which the wenches say is a gallimaufry of gambols, because they are not in it. But they themselves are o' the mind – if it be not too rough for some that know little but bowling – it will please plentifully.

The Winter's Tale, iv.3.

[Half-a-dozen shepherds' families inhabited Stratford, two of them in Henley Street, opposite Shakespeare's early home; and another lodged with the Hathaways at Shottery.]

So many days my ewes have been with young,
So many weeks before the poor fools will ean [lamb],
So many years ere I shall shear the fleece . . .
Gives not the hawthorn bush a sweeter shade
To shepherds looking on their silly sheep . . .
       the shepherd's homely curds,
His cold thin drink out of his leather bottle,
His wonted sleep under a fresh tree's shade . . .

3 Henry VI, ii.5.

The nine men's morris is filled up with mud,
And the quaint mazes in the wanton green
Are for lack of tread undistinguishable.

A Midsummer Night's Dream, ii.1.

As a pancake for Shrove Tuesday, a morris for Mayday.
All's Well That Ends Well, ii.2.

He that sets up his rest to do more exploits with his mace than a morris-pike.
The Comedy of Errors, iv.3.

I have seen
Him caper upright like a wild Morisco.
2 Henry VI, iii.1.

[It is nice to think that morris-dancing never died out in the Cotswolds, and historically appropriate that it was from there that it was generally revived in our time.]

Some say the lark and loathèd toad change eyes.
Romeo and Juliet, iii.5.

Didst thou not fall out with a tailor for wearing his new doublet before Easter?
Romeo and Juliet, iii.1.

The spinsters and the knitters in the sun,
And the free maids that weave their thread with bones
Do use to chant it.
Twelfth Night, ii.4.

So bees with smoke and doves with stench
Are from their hives and houses driven away.
1 Henry VI, i.5.

Or like a lazy thresher with a flail.
3 Henry VI, ii.1.

Hard as the palm of ploughman.
Troilus and Cressida, i.1.

Thunder shall not so awake the beds of eels.
Pericles, iv.2.

What time the shepherd blowing of his nails.
3 Henry VI, ii.5.

When icicles hang by the wall,
　　And Dick the shepherd blows his nail,
And Tom bears logs into the hall,
　　And milk comes frozen home in pail;
When blood is nipped, and ways be foul,
Then nightly sings the staring owl . . .

When all aloud the wind doth blow,
　　And coughing drowns the parson's saw,
And birds sit brooding in the snow,
　　And Marian's nose looks red and raw;
When roasted crabs hiss in the bowl,
Then nightly sings the staring owl . . .

*　　*　　*

When daisies pied and violets blue
　　And lady-smocks all silver-white,
And cuckoo-buds of yellow hue
　　Do paint the meadows with delight;
The cuckoo then, on every tree,
Mocks married men; for thus sings he – Cuckoo.

When shepherds pipe on oaten straws,
　　And merry larks are ploughmen's clocks,
When turtles tread, and rooks, and daws,
　　And maidens bleach their summer smocks . . .

Love's Labour's Lost, v.2.

[Quiller-Couch, himself a creative writer, saw that, rather than from books, 'it is even more likely that he brought all this fairy stuff up to London in his own head, packed with nursery legends of his native Warwickshire. When will criticism learn to allow for the enormous drafts made by creative artists such as Shakespeare and Dickens upon their childhood?' QED.]

Places He Knew

In Warwickshire I have true-hearted friends.

3 Henry VI, iv.8.

And as the butcher takes away the calf,
And binds the wretch, and beats it when it strays,
Bearing it to the bloody slaughter-house . . .
And as the dam runs lowing up and down,
Looking the way her harmless young one went.

2 Henry VI, iii.1.

[A familiar scene in the streets of Stratford. Remember that Shakespeare's father was a glover. John Aubrey was not so far off in saying a 'butcher', for of course a glover would take part in the slaughter of animals. This play is one of Shakespeare's very earliest, when he was not far away from those scenes.]

I saw a smith stand with his hammer, thus,
The whilst his iron did on the anvil cool,
With open mouth swallowing a tailor's news:
Who, with his shears and measure in his hand,
Standing on slippers – which his nimble haste
Had falsely thrust upon contràry feet –
Told of a many thousand warlike French
That were embattled and ranked in Kent.
Another lean unwashed artificer
Cuts off his tale.

King John, iv.2.

[Another veracious scene from Stratford, for we know that Hornsby the

106

smith lived in Henley Street; a tailor lived round the corner. The scene carries the conviction of one observed.]

This is the forest of Arden; aye, now am I in Arden.

As You Like It, ii.4.

Am not I Christopher Sly, old Sly's son of Burton-heath [Barton on the Heath][1] . . . Ask Marian Hacket, the fat ale-wife of Wincot [near Stratford] . . .

Nor no such men as you have reckoned up,
As Stephen Sly and old John Naps of Greet.[2]

The Taming of the Shrew, Induction, 2.

Full many a glorious morning have I seen
Flatter the mountain-tops with sovereign eye,
Kissing with golden face the meadows green,
Gilding pale streams with heavenly alchemy.

Sonnet 33

[Elizabethans were apt to describe hills as mountains, and so the familiar ridge of the Cotswolds appears from the meadows and streams of Stratford.]

How does your fallow greyhound, sir? I heard say he was outrun on Cotsall [Cotswold].

The Merry Wives of Windsor, i.1.

You Banbury cheese!

Ibid.

What a devil dost thou in Warwickshire? I thought your honour had already been at Shrewsbury.

1 Henry IV, iv.2.

Do you mean to stop any of William's wages, about the sack he lost the other day at Hinckley Fair? . . . I beseech you, sir, to countenance William Visor of Wincot against Clement Perks of the Hill.

2 Henry IV, v.1.

---

[1] Where Shakespeare's uncle and aunt, the Lamberts, lived.
[2] Across the Cotswolds in Gloucestershire.

By'r Lady, I think 'a be but goodman Puff of Barson.

2 Henry IV, v.3.

[i.e. Barcheston in Warwickshire, where Sheldon tapestries were made.]

I dare say my cousin William is become a good scholar. He is at Oxford still, is he not? . . .

I was once of Clement's Inn. There was I, and little John Doit of Staffordshire and black George Barnes and Francis Pickbone, and Will Squele a Cotswold man. You had not four such swinge-bucklers in all the Inns of Court again . . . That same Sir John, I saw him break Skogan's head at the court-gate, and the very same day did I fight with one Sampson Stockfish, a fruiterer, behind Gray's Inn . . .

How a good yoke of bullocks at Stamford Fair? . . . O, Sir John, do you remember how we lay all night in the windmill in St George's Fields? . . .

I remember at Mile End Green, when I lay at Clement's Inn – I was then Sir Dagonet in Arthur's show – there was a little quiver fellow, and 'a would manage you his piece thus . . .

And now is this Vice's dagger become a squire, and talks as familiarly of John a Gaunt as if he had been sworn brother to him. And I'll be sworn 'a never saw him but once in the Tilt Yard [at Westminster].

2 Henry IV, iii.2.

I will make a Star Chamber matter of it: if he were twenty Sir John Falstaffs, he shall not abuse Robert Shallow, esquire. In the county of Gloucester, Justice of the Peace, and *coram*. Aye, and *custolorum*.

The Merry Wives of Windsor, i.1.

[i.e. of the *quorum*, the specially selected J.P.s, and *custos rotulorum*, keeper of the rolls.]

Get thee before to Coventry . . . our soldiers shall march through – we'll to Sutton Co'fil [Coldfield] tonight . . .

No eye hath seen such scarecrows. I'll not march through Coventry with them, that's flat. There's but a shirt and a half in all my company . . . and the shirt, to say the truth, stolen from my host at St Albans, or the red-nose innkeeper of Daventry.

1 Henry IV, iv.2.

How far hence is thy lord, mine honest fellow?
– By this at Dunsmore, marching hitherward . . .
How far off is our brother Montagu?
– By this at Daintry [Daventry] with a puissant troop.
And, by thy guess, how nigh is Clarence now?
– At Southam I did leave him with his forces . . .
The drum your honour hears marcheth from Warwick.

3 Henry VI, v.1.

[Along Watling Street, direct route between London and Stratford.]

How far is it . . . to Berkeley now? . . .
I am a stranger here in Gloucestershire,
These high wild hills and rough uneven ways
Draw out our miles and make them wearisome . . .
            what a weary way
From Ravenspurgh to Cotswold will be found.

Richard II, ii.3.

I hope to see London once ere I die.

2 Henry IV, v.3.

This is some priory – In, or we are spoiled! . . .

Come this way to the melancholy vale,
The place of death and sorry execution,
Behind the ditches of the abbey here.

The Comedy of Errors, v.1.

[The American Shakespearean scholar, T. F. Baldwin, pointed out that the earliest theatres, the Theatre and Curtain, where Shakespeare's early plays were performed, were built in the purlieus of Holywell priory, and in the vale were the gibbets where hangings took place. This play was one of the earliest.]

The bells of St Bennet may put you in mind – one, two, three.

Twelfth Night, v.1.

[St Bennet, Paul's Wharf, was just across the Thames from the Globe – nice to think of that attentive ear listening to the bells.]

Meet me tomorrow at the Temple hall.

1 Henry IV, iii.3.

[Middle Temple hall was the scene of a performance of *Twelfth Night* in February 1602.]

> In the south suburbs at 'The Elephant'
> Is best to lodge.
>
> *Twelfth Night*, III.3.

[At this very time an inn called 'The Elephant' existed in Southwark, near the Globe Theatre.]

> Meet me tomorrow in St George's field.
>
> *2 Henry VI*, V.1.

[Also in Southwark.]

> As common as the way between St Albans and London.
>
> *2 Henry IV*, II.2.

> Inquire at London, 'mongst the taverns there:
> For there, they say, he daily doth frequent
> With unrestrained loose companions.
>
> *Richard II*, V.3.

> Would I were in an alehouse in London.
>
> *Henry V*, III.2.

> – thou laid'st a trap to take my life
> As well at London Bridge as at the Tower.
>
> *1 Henry VI*, III.1.

> Away, away, aboard! Thy master is shipped, and thou art to post after with oars . . . Away, you'll lose the tide if you tarry any longer.
>
> *The Two Gentlemen of Verona*, II.3.

[It was necessary to catch the tide to shoot under the arches of London Bridge.]

> Ne'er through an arch so hurried the blown tide.
>
> *Coriolanus*, V.4.

As I have seen a swan
With bootless labour swim against the tide,
And spend her strength with over-matching waves.

3 Henry VI, i.4.

the swan's down-feather
That stands upon the swell at full of tide,
And neither way inclines.

Antony and Cleopatra, iii.2.

This is the way
To Julius Caesar's ill-erected Tower.

Richard II, v.1.

I do not like the Tower, of any place:
Did Julius Caesar build that place, my lord?
– He did, my gracious lord, begin that place,
Which, since, succeeding ages have re-edified.
– Is it upon record, or else reported,
Successively from age to age, he built it?

Richard III, iii.1.

[So Elizabethans believed, *cf.* my *Tower of London*.]

I'll to the Tower with all the haste I can
To view the artillery and munitiòn.
– To Eltham will I, where the young king is.

1 Henry VI, i.1.

And smell like Bucklersbury in simple-time . . . Thou mightest as
well say, I like to walk by the Counter-gate,[1] which is as hateful to
me as the reek of a lime-kiln.

The Merry Wives of Windsor, iii.3.

He's gone into Smithfield to buy your worship a horse.
– I bought him in Paul's, and he'll buy me a horse in Smithfield.

2 Henry IV, i.2.

This oily rascal is known as well as Paul's.

1 Henry IV, ii.4.

[1] There were three of these prisons for debtors in the City, and one in Southwark.

[Old St Paul's Cathedral, bigger than the present one, dominated the City.]

> Unless we sweep 'em from the door with cannons . . . We may as
> well push against Paul's as stir 'em . . .
> – Is this Moorfields to muster in? Or have we some strange Indian
> with the great tool come to Court, the women so besiege us?
> – These are the youths that thunder at a playhouse, and fight for
> bitten apples – that no audience but the Tribulation of Tower Hill,
> or the Limbs of Limehouse, are able to endure . . .
> Go, break among the press, and find a way out
> To let the troop pass fairly, or I'll find
> A Marshalsea shall hold ye play these two months.
>
> *Henry VIII*, v.4.

> Thou makest the triumviry, the corner cap of society,
> The shape of love's Tyburn, that hangs up simplicity.
>
> *Love's Labour's Lost*, iv.3.

[The gallows at Tyburn, on the way to Paddington, were set triangularly, like an academic corner cap.]

> The most convenient place that I can think of
> For such receipt of learning is Blackfriars.
>
> *Henry VIII*, ii.2.

> And presently repair to Crosby Place,
> . . . after I have solemnly interred
> At Chertsey monastery this noble king . . .
> – Toward Chertsey, noble lord?
> No: to White-Friars. There attend my coming.
>
> *Richard III*, i.2.

[Crosby Place in Bishopsgate, where Richard planned his *coup d'état*, was familiar to Shakespeare, for at one time he lodged in the parish. Since removed to Chelsea.]

> You must no more call it York Place: that's past;
> For since the Cardinal fell, that title's lost:
> 'Tis now the King's, and called Whitehall.
>
> *Henry VIII*, iv.1.

Methought I sat in seat of majesty
In the cathedral church of Westminster,
And in that chair where kings and queens are crowned.
2 Henry VI, i.2.

Doth any name particular belong
Unto the lodging where I first did swound? –
– Tis called Jerusalem, my noble lord.
– Laud be to God! even there my life must end.
It hath been prophesied to me many years
I should not die but in Jerusalem,
Which vainly I supposed the Holy Land.
But bear me to that Chamber: there I'll lie:
In that Jerusalem shall Harry die.
2 Henry IV, iv.5.

[Jerusalem chamber, at the west end of Westminster Abbey.]

Tomorrow morning by four o'clock, early at Gadshill! There are
pilgrims going to Canterbury with rich offerings, and traders riding
to London with fat purses. Gadshill lies tonight in Rochester; I have
bespoke supper tomorrow night in East-Cheap. – Meet me
tomorrow night in East-Cheap.
1 Henry IV, i.2.

[Rochester, an inn-yard.]

Heigh-ho! An't be not four by the day I'll be hanged: Charles's wain
is over the new chimney, and yet our horse not packed . . .
I think this be the most villainous house in all London Road for
fleas . . .
I have a gammon of bacon and two razes [roots] of ginger to be
delivered as far as Charing Cross . . .
Sirrah carrier, what time do you mean to come to London?
– Time enough to go to bed with a candle.
1 Henry IV, ii.1.

The best courtier of them all when the Court lay at Windsor, could
never have brought her to such a canary [quandary].
The Merry Wives of Windsor, ii.2.

Go you through the town to Frogmore . . . Go about the fields with
me to Frogmore . . .
Marry, sir, the Petty Ward, the Park Ward, every way; Old
Windsor way, and every way but the town way . . .
Hear mine host of 'the Garter' . . .
Your husband's coming hither, with all the officers of Windsor, to
search for a gentleman that he says is here now in the house . . . Go
take up these clothes here quickly . . . Carry them to the laundress
in Datchet Mead.

There is an old tale goes that Herne the Hunter,
Sometime a keeper here in Windsor Forest,
Doth all the wintertime, at still midnight,
Walk round about an oak, with great ragged horns.
And there he blasts the tree and takes the cattle,
And makes milch-kine yield blood, and shakes a chain
In a most hideous and dreadful manner.
You have heard of such a spirit, and well you know
The superstitious idle-headed eld
Received and did deliver to our age
The tale of Herne the Hunter for a truth . . .
Why, yet there want not many that do fear
In deep of night to walk by this Herne's Oak.
                    The Merry Wives of Windsor, iv.4.

Her father hath commanded her to slip
Away with Slender, and with him at Eton
Immediately to marry . . .
And at the deanery where a priest attends . . .

I came yonder at Eton to marry Mistress Anne Page, and she's a
great lubberly boy: if it had not been in the church, I would have
swinged him.
                    The Merry Wives of Windsor, v.5.

Cricket, to Windsor chimneys shalt thou leap:
Where fires thou find'st unraked and hearths unswept,
There pinch the maids as blue as blueberry:
Our radiant Queen hates sluts and sluttery . . .
Search Windsor Castle, elves, within and out:
Strew good luck, ouphs, on every sacred room,
That it may stand till the perpetual doom,

In state as wholesome as in state 'tis fit,
Worthy the owner and the owner it.
The several chairs of Order look you scour
With juice of balm and every precious flower:
Each fair instalment, coat and several crest,
With loyal blazon evermore be blest!
And nightly, meadow fairies, look you sing,
Like to the Garter's compass in a ring:
The expressure that it bears, green let it be,
More fertile-fresh than all the field to see.
And *Honi soit qui mal y pense* write
In emerald tufts, flowers purple, blue and white;
Like sapphire, pearl and rich embroidery,
Buckled below fair knighthood's bending knee . . .
Away, disperse! But till 'tis one o'clock,
Our dance of custom round about the oak
Of Herne the Hunter, let us not forget.

Ibid.

Goose, if I had you upon Sarum Plain,
I'd drive ye cackling home to Camelot.

King Lear, ii.2.

[Geese were a feature of the open spaces of Salisbury Plain. Elizabethans thought of Winchester as Arthurian Camelot.]

Those twins of learning that he raised in you,
Ipswich and Oxford! One of which fell with him . . .
The other, though unfinished, yet so famous,
So excellent in art, and still so rising.[1]

Henry VIII, iv.2.

Know'st thou the way to Dover?
− Both stile and gate, horse-way and footpath . . .
Thou wilt o'ertake us, hence a mile or twain
In the way to Dover.

King Lear, iv.1.

[1] This refers to Christ Church. Oxford was familiar ground, on one route between Stratford and London.

How fearful,
And dizzy 'tis to cast one's eye so low!
The crows and choughs that wing the midway air
Show scarce so gross as beetles; halfway down
Hangs one that gathers samphire, dreadful trade! . . .
The fishermen that walk upon the beach
Appear like mice, and yon tall anchoring bark
Diminished to her cock, her cock a buoy
Almost too small for sight. The murmuring surge
That on the unnumbered idle pebbles chafes
Cannot be heard so high.

King Lear, iv.6.

[Shakespeare's cliff at Dover is appropriately commemorative, for his
Company, by now the King's Men, played in Dover, 30 August 1606.
King Lear was performed at Court 26 December 1606. This gives us a
date for the play, written that autumn.]

The Court

ༀ

But now thy uncle is removing hence,
As princes do their Courts when they are cloyed
With long continuance in a settled place.

1 Henry VI, ii.5.

[This was the regular routine with Elizabeth I, somewhat restless.]

And now what rests but that we spend the time
With stately triumphs, mirthful comic shows,
Such as befit the pleasure of the Court?

3 Henry VI, v.7.

The Court's a learning place.

All's Well That Ends Well, i.1.

Clown: I know my business is but to the Court.
Countess: Why, what place make you special, when you put off that
with such contempt? – 'But to the Court'!
Clown: Truly, madam, if God have lent a man any manners, he may
easily put it off at Court. He that cannot make a leg, put off his cap,
kiss his hand, and say nothing, has neither leg, hands, lip, nor cap.
And, indeed, such a fellow, to say precisely, were not for the Court.

All's Well That Ends Well, ii.2.

The art of the Court –
As hard to leave as keep – whose top to climb
Is certain falling, or so slippery that
The fear's as bad as falling.

Cymbeline, iii.3.

117

I hear of none but the new proclamation
That's clapped upon the Court-gate.
          . . . What is it for?
The reformation of our travelled gallants
That fill the Court with quarrels, talk, and tailors.
Henry VIII, i.3.

Virginity, like an old courtier, wears her cap out of fashion.
All's Well That Ends Well, i.1.

[Like old Burghley.]

This might be the pate of a politician . . . one that would circumvent
God . . . Or of a courtier, which could say, 'Good morrow, sweet
lord! How dost thou, good lord?' This might be my Lord Such-a-one,
that praised my Lord Such-a-one's horse, when he meant to beg it.
Hamlet, v.1.

          Consider,
When you above perceive me like a crow
That it is place which lessens and sets off;
And you may then revolve what tales I have told you
Of Courts, of princes, of the tricks in war . . .
          O, this life
Is nobler than attending for a check,
Richer than doing nothing for a bribe,
Prouder than rustling in unpaid-for silk –
Such gain the cap of him that makes 'em fine,
Yet keeps his book uncrossed. No life to ours.
Cymbeline, iii.3.

Hath not old custom made this life more sweet
Than that of painted pomp? Are not these woods
More free from peril than the envious Court?
As You Like It, ii.1.

          Not a courtier –
Although they wear their faces to the bent
Of the king's looks – hath a heart that is not
Glad at the thing they scowl at.
Cymbeline, i.1.

Why, if thou never wast at court, thou never sawest good manners . . .
– Not a whit . . . those that are good manners at the Court are as ridiculous in the country as the behaviour of the country is most mockable at the Court . . . You salute not at the Court, but you kiss your hands: that courtesy would be uncleanly if courtiers were shepherds . . . We are still [always] handling our ewes, and their fells, you know, are greasy.
Why, do not your courtier's hands sweat? And is not the grease of a mutton as wholesome as the sweat of a man? . . .
– They are often tarred over with the surgery of our sheep. The courtier's hands are perfumed with civet.
Civet is of a baser birth than tar, the very uncleanly flux of a cat.

As You Like It, iii.2.

I cannot tell for which of his virtues it was, but he was certainly whipped out of the Court.
– His vices you would say: there's no virtue whipped out of the Court: they cherish it, to make it stay there, and yet it will no more but abide.

The Winter's Tale, iv.2.

Are you a courtier, an't like you, sir?
– Whether it like me or no, I am a courtier. Seest thou not the air of the Court in these enfoldings? Hath not my gait in it the measure of the Court? Receives not thy nose Court-odour from me? Reflect I not on thy baseness Court-contempt? . . . I am courtier, cap-a-pe, and one that will either push on or pluck back thy business there.

The Winter's Tale, iv.3.

And how like you this shepherd's life?
– . . . In respect that it is in the fields, it pleaseth me well; but in respect it is not in the Court, it is tedious.

As You Like It, iii.2.

Lord, who would live turmoiled in the Court,
And may enjoy such quiet walks as these?
This small inheritance my father left me
Contenteth me, and worth a monarchy.
I seek not to wax great by others' waning,
Or gather wealth I care not with what envy:

Sufficeth that I have maintains my state,
And sends the poor well pleasèd from my gate.

2 Henry VI, iv.10.

[Shakespeare's Company – the Lord Chamberlain's, subsequently taken under James I's patronage as the King's Men – was the premier favourite for performances at Court, where courtiers would be sophisticated enough to enjoy jokes at their expense. Frequent performances at Court would give him an acquaintance with characters and events there.]

He hath been a courtier he swears.
– I have trod a measure [dance]; I have flattered a lady; I have been politic with my friend, smooth with my enemy; I have undone three tailors; I have had four quarrels, and like to have fought one.

As You Like It, v.4.

Elizabeth I and James I

🦎

Thou remember'st
Since once I sat upon a promontory,
And heard a mermaid on a dolphin's back . . .
That very time I saw, but thou could'st not,
Flying between the cold moon and the earth,
Cupid all armed. A certain aim he took
At a fair Vestal thronèd by the west,
And loosed his love-shaft smartly from his bow,
As it should pierce a hundred thousand hearts.
But I might see young Cupid's fiery shaft
Quenched in the chaste beams of the watery moon,
And the imperial votaress passed on
In maiden meditation, fancy-free.

A Midsummer Night's Dream, ii.1.

[This refers back to the famous Entertainments laid on by Leicester at nearby Kenilworth in 1575, in his last attempt to press the Queen into marrying him. The Castle was then practically surrounded by a large lake, on which water-pageants were a feature. Hence the reference – and the rôle of Cupid too: the neighbourhood would retain some knowledge of the purpose of these spectacular entertainments. Nor is it improbable that an observant boy of eleven was among the country people who flocked in to see them. An early stage-direction in *Henry VI* uniquely gives 'on the terrace' at Kenilworth, which he would have known.]

Where I have come, great clerks have purposèd
To greet me with premeditated welcomes;
Where I have seen them shiver and look pale,
Make periods in the midst of sentences,

121

> Throttle their practised accent in their fears,
> And in conclusion dumbly have broke off,
> Not paying me a welcome.
>> *A Midsummer Night's Dream*, v.1.

[The Queen paid a visit to Oxford in 1592, attended by the Court, among them young Southampton, who was created an M.A. on the occasion. No reason why the Earl's poet should not have been in attendance – on the familiar road between Stratford and London. Just such a breakdown of a don in the midst of his oration as here described has been recorded.]

> And there is such confusion in my powers
> As, after some oration fairly spoke
> By a belovèd prince, there doth appear,
> Among the buzzing pleasèd multitude –
> Where every something, being blent together,
> Turns to a wild of nothing, save of joy,
> Expressed and not expressed.
>> *The Merchant of Venice*, III.2.

[The Queen herself was an impressive orator on public occasions, such as the opening of Parliament.]

> As on the finger of a thronèd queen
> The basest jewel will be well esteemed.
>> Sonnet 96

[Frequent performances before her gave Shakespeare plenty of opportunities of observing her close at hand; *cf.* the following.]

> Like vassalage at unawares encount'ring
> The eye of majesty.
>> *Troilus and Cressida*, III.2.

> Cricket, to Windsor chimneys shalt thou leap:
> Where fires thou find'st unraked and hearths unswept,
> There pinch the maids as blue as bilberry,
> Our radiant Queen hates sluts and sluttery.
>> *The Merry Wives of Windsor*, v.5.

[The Court was frequently at Windsor, familiar ground to Shakespeare.]

This royal infant – heaven still move about her! –
Though in her cradle, yet now promises
Upon this land a thousand thousand blessings,
Which time shall bring to ripeness. She shall be –
But few now living can behold that goodness –
A pattern to all princes living with her,
And all that shall suceed. Saba was never
More covetous of wisdom and fair virtue
Than this pure soul shall be. All princely graces
That mould up such a mighty piece as this is,
With all the virtues that attend the good,
Shall still be doubled on her. Truth shall nurse her;
Holy and heavenly thoughts still counsel her.
She shall be loved and feared; her own shall bless her;
Her foes shake like a field of beaten corn,
And hang their head with sorrow. Good grows with her,
In her days every man shall eat in safety
Under his own vine what he plants, and sing
The merry songs of peace to all his neighbours.
God shall be truly known, and those about her
From her shall read the perfect ways of honour,
And by those claim their greatness, not by blood . . .
She shall be, to the happiness of England,
An agèd princess; many days shall see her,
And yet no day without a deed to crown it.

Henry VIII, v.5.

[This famous speech – Archbishop Cranmer's prophecy at his christening of the infant Princess Elizabeth – was written into *Henry VIII*,
Shakespeare's last play, 1612, when the triumph of her reign could be
seen in some perspective.]

Our fears in Banquo
Stick deep, and in his royalty of nature
Reigns that which would be feared . . .
And to that dauntless temper of his mind
He hath a wisdom that doth guide his valour
To act in safety . . .
He chid the sisters
When first they put the name of King upon me . . .

> Then prophet-like
> They hailed him father to a line of Kings . . .
>
> *Macbeth*, iii.1.

> *A show of eight Kings, Ghost of Banquo following.*
> What, will the line stretch out to the crack of doom? . . .
> And yet the eighth appears, who bears a glass
> Which shows me many more; and some
> That two-fold balls and treble sceptres carry, I see
>
> *Macbeth*, iv.1.

[It is well known that *Macbeth* was written in compliment to James I, after the fright the country received in 1605 from Gunpowder Plot, to which there are indirect references in the play. And Banquo was the putative ancestor of the Stuart line. The 'two-fold balls and treble sceptres' is a specific reference to James as king of both England and Scotland; the treble sceptre refers to France to which English kings laid claim. It always appeared in the royal title until George III gave it up in 1763.]

> Even so
> The general [populace], subject to a well-wished king,
> Quit their own part, and in obsequious fondness
> Crowd to his presence, where their untaught love
> Must needs appear offence.
>
> *Measure for Measure*, ii.4.

> I love the people,
> But do not like to stage me to their eyes.
> Though it do well, I do not relish well
> Their loud applause and Aves vehement,
> Nor do I think the man of safe discretion
> That does affect it.
>
> *Measure for Measure*, i.1.

[On James I's accession in 1603 he was greeted by crowds on his progress into England – a proclamation was put forth restraining resort to the new monarch, who did not relish playing to the gallery as Elizabeth I had done with such success. Note the preciseness of 'a well-wished king': James's peaceful accession put an end to the uncertainty and anxiety with regard to the succession to the Crown that clouded Elizabeth I's last years. And Essex sympathisers lookedforward to it with too keen anticipation. *Measure for Measure* of 1604 reflects the new situation.]

> Comes the king forth? . . .
> – Ay, sir, there are a crew of wretched souls
> That stay his cure. Their malady convinces
> The great assay of art; but at his touch,
> Such sanctity hath heaven given his hand,
> They presently amend . . .
> What's the disease he means?
>   'Tis called the Evil.
> A most miraculous work in this good king,
> Which often, since my here-remain in England,
> I have seen him do. How he solicits heaven
> Himself best knows; but strangely-visited people,
> All swollen and ulcerous, pitiful to the eye,
> The mere despair of surgery, he cures;
> Hanging a golden stamp about their necks,
> Put on with holy prayers. And 'tis spoken
> To the succeeding royalty he leaves
> The healing benediction. With this strange virtue
> He hath a heavenly gift of prophecy,
> And sundry blessings hang about his throne
> That speak him full of grace.

Macbeth, IV.3.

[*Macbeth* appeared early in 1606, a tribute to James I, who after some hesitation – and a Calvinist upbringing – decided to continue the sacramental power of kingship in touching for the King's Evil, scrofula or scurvy. The Stuarts continued to employ this attribute of monarchy, up to the last of them, Queen Anne, who 'touched' Dr Johnson as a boy – without noticeable effect, except reinforcing his reverence for monarchy.

James I rewarded the players well, taking Shakespeare's Company under his patronage as the King's Men, doubling their remuneration for performances at Court, and constituting the Fellows of the Company Grooms of the Chamber with an allowance.

At the end of *Cymbeline*, written 1609–10, Philarmonus a soothsayer reads and interprets an oracle from Jupiter:

'Whereas a lion's whelp shall . . . be embraced by a piece of tender air [mollis aer, i.e. mulier, a woman]; and when from a stately cedar shall be lopped branches which being dead many years, shall after revive, be jointed to the old stock and freshly grow . . . then shall Britain be fortunate and flourish in peace and plenty.'

He interprets 'the piece of tender air' to Cymbeline as 'My virtuous daughter'. Then,

> The lofty cedar, royal Cymbeline,
> Personates thee;

the branches lopped, Cymbeline's two lost sons now found:

> whose issue
> Promises Britain peace and plenty.

All this is a graceful tribute, in Shakespear's indirect, tactful manner to James I, who had taken Shakespeare's Company under his patronage. Cymbeline has two sons, as James I has, Prince Henry and Prince Charles; Cymbeline has an only daughter, as James has in the Princess Elizabeth – ultimate ancestress of our present royal line.

It is all a tribute to the new dynasty, the Stuarts, 'jointed to the old stock', the Tudors. In the play the action converges improbably upon Milford Haven. Why? – Because there James's ancestor, Henry VII, had landed from whom came James's claim to the throne. His reign, as *Rex pacificus*, was indeed a time of peace and plenty after long war.

An old record states that Sir William Davenant had in his possession a letter of King James to his dramatist. There is no reason why this should not be true. The historian knows how much disappears in the course of time. It is remarkable that, contrary to popular opinion, we know more about William Shakespeare than about any other Elizabethan dramatist.]

> As when
> The bird of wonder dies, the maiden phoenix,
> Her ashes new-create another heir
> As great in admiration [wonder] as herself,
> So shall she leave her blessedness to one . . .
> Who from the sacred ashes of her honour,
> Shall star-like rise, as great in fame as she was,
> And so stand fixed. Peace, plenty, love, truth, terror . . .
> Shall then be his, and like a vine grow to him.

His honour and the greatness of his name
Shall be, and make new nations. He shall flourish
And, like a mountain cedar, reach his branches
To all the plains about him. Our children's children
Shall see this, and bless heaven.

Henry VIII, v.5.

[This tribute to James I continues from that to Elizabeth I in Cranmer's prophecy at her christening. The interesting feature in it is the reference to the creation of 'new nations', i.e. Virginia, from the foundation of Jamestown in 1607. The 'mountain cedar' there features in Hakluyt and Ralegh's writings about it – Shakespeare typically picked it up, as his mind picked up everything.]

Contemporary Persons

୧

So is it not with me as with that Muse,
Stirred by a painted beauty to his verse,
Who heaven itself for ornament doth use
And every fair with his fair doth rehearse;
Making a couplement of proud compare
With sun and moon, and earth and sea's rich gems,
With April's first-born flowers, and all things rare
That heaven's air in this huge rondure hems.

Sonnet 21

[Sir Philip Sidney and Penelope, Lady Rich, in *Astrophil and Stella*, 1591: her brilliant complexion, perhaps painted, was her strong point. Shakespeare apparently did not like painted women or false hair.]

Great princes' favourites their fair leaves spread
But as the marigold at the sun's eye,
And in themselves their pride lies buried,
For at a frown they in their glory die.
The painful warrior famousèd for fight,
After a thousand victories once foiled,
Is from the book of honour razèd quite,
And all the rest forgot for which he toiled.

Sonnet 25

[This refers to the fall of Sir Walter Ralegh in 1592, his characteristics recognisably described: his fame as a warrior; 'painful' meant 'painstaking', and he was notoriously industrious. At this very moment Robert Cecil was writing, 'he can toil terribly'. The date of the sonnet is 1592.]

128

For what care I who calls me well or ill,
So you o'er*green* [Greene] my bad, my good allow?

Sonnet 112

The thrice three Muses mourning for the death
Of Learning late deceased in beggary.

A Midsummer Night's Dream, v.1.

[Greene died in squalor and penury in 1592. Shakespeare referred to the university wits, such as Marlowe, as the 'learned' with respect for their 'learning'.]

This Armado is a Spaniard that keeps here in Court.

Love's Labour's Lost, iv.1.

Our Court, you know, is haunted
With a refinèd traveller of Spain;
A man in all the world's new fashion planted,
That hath a mint of phrases in his brain.
One whom the music of his own vain tongue
Doth ravish like enchanting harmony;
A man of compliments, whom right and wrong
Have chose as umpire of their mutiny . . .
A man of fire-new words, fashion's own knight.
But, I protest, I love to hear him lie,
And I will use him for my minstrelsy.

Love's Labour's Lost, i.1.

Armado: Sir, the King is a noble gentleman, and my familiar – I do assure ye – very good friend. For what is inward between us, let it pass . . . I must tell you, it will please his grace, by the world, sometime to lean upon my poor shoulder, and with his royal finger thus dally with my excrement, my mustachio – but, sweet heart, let that pass.

Love's Labour's Lost, v.1.

[We know that in this private play, a skit on Southampton's circle, the King stood for Southampton, Berowne for Shakespeare, Don Armado for Antonio Pérez. As Secretary of State to Philip II he had been very intimate with the King, who, it was noted, would take him along with him alone in his coach. In exile Pérez would not fail to boast of his intimacy with the monarch. He was at this time put up by Essex at Essex House, only too well known to all Essex's circle, in which Southampton figured. Pérez is caricatured throughout this Southampton play by his poet.]

> *Polonius:* And these few precepts in thy memory
> Look thou charàcter . . .
>
> *Hamlet* I.3.

> *Polonius:* Hath there been such a time – I'd fain know that –
> That I have positively said, 'Tis so',
> When it proved otherwise?
> *King:*　　　　　　　　Not that I know.
> *Polonius:* Take this from this, if this be otherwise.
> (*Pointing to his head and shoulder.*)
>
> *Hamlet,* II.2.

> *Hamlet:* The satirical rogue says here that old men have grey beards, that their faces are wrinkled, their eyes purging thick amber and plum-tree gum; and that they have a plentiful lack of wit, together with most weak hams.
>
> *Ibid.*

[Shakespeare's personal affiliation had been with Southampton, Essex's chief follower; they were opposed to the Queen's minister, Lord Burghley. To anyone who knows Burghley's characteristics in old age, Polonius is a recognisable caricature. He had died in 1598 – so it was safe to caricature him – leaving his famous Precepts for his son, which are guyed. His intelligence system is pinpointed in Polonius' spying, both on Laertes and on Hamlet. As chief minister, he is indispensable, always right, and prosy, as Burghley became. In old age Burghley was always complaining of his rheumy eyes – 'I am but as a monoculus', etc., – and weak hams, which made him take to riding a mule about his gardens, as in the Bodleian portrait.]

> You would have thought the very windows spake,
> So many greedy looks of young and old
> Through casements darted their desiring eyes
> Upon his visage . . .
> Whilst he, from one side to the other turning,
> Bare-headed, lower than his proud steed's neck
> Bespake them thus, 'I thank you, countrymen.'
>
> *Richard II*, v.2.

Ourself . . .
Observed his courtship of the common people:
How he did seem to dive into their hearts
With humble and familiar courtesy
What reverence he did throw away on slaves
Wooing poor craftsmen with the craft of smiles,
And patient underbearing of his fortune . . .
Oft goes his bonnet to an oyster-wench;
A brace of draymen bid God speed him well,
And had the tribute of his supple knee,
With 'Thanks, my countrymen, my loving friends.'
As were our England in reversion his,
And he our subjects' next degree in hope.

Richard II, i.4.

[Essex's cult of popularity, which challenged the Queen's, became more and more a subject of distrust with her and built up a grievance. It was not that he aimed at the succession to the throne, but he certainly aimed at controlling it, an unforgiven incursion into the *arcana imperii*.]

How London doth pour out her citizens!
The mayor and all his brethren in best sort,
Like to the senators of the antique Rome,
With the plebians swarming at their heels,
Go forth and fetch their conquering Caesar in.
– As by a lower but loving likelihood
Were now the General of our gracious Empress,
As in good time he may, from Ireland coming,
Bringing rebellion broachèd on his sword,
How many would the peaceful city quit
To welcome him!

Henry V, v. Chorus

[Essex had a great send-off from London on leaving in 1599 to crush O'Neill's rebellion – one observes the expectancy, which was disappointed.]

The courtier's, soldier's, scholar's, eye, tongue, sword,
The expectancy and rose of the fair state,
The glass of fashion, and the mould of form,
The observed of all observers.

Hamlet, iii.1.

[Essex described sympathetically, and recognisably, for he had precisely those gifts, was well educated, the most popular figure in the firmament of the Court, and such were the popular expectations of him.]

> like favourites,
> Made proud by princes, that advance their pride
> Against that power that bred it.
>
> *Much Ado About Nothing*, III.1.

[Essex's opposition to the Queen: the situation as it was in 1599, the date of the play. One sees Shakespeare's opinion of Essex changing with his unstable, dangerous course.]

> He is so plaguy-proud that the death-tokens of it
> Cry 'No recovery'.
>
> *Troilus and Cressida*, II.3.

> 'Tis certain greatness, once fallen out with fortune,
> Must fall out with men too: what the declined is
> He shall as soon read in the eyes of others
> As feel in his own fall . . .
> Which when they fall, as being slippery standers,
> The love that leaned on them as slippery too,
> Do one pluck down another, and together die in the fall.
>
> *Troilus and Cressida*, III.3.

[This reflects the recent fall of Essex, Francis Bacon having been the first to desert Essex and go over to the other side.]

> The great man down, you mark his favourite flies,
> The poor advanced makes friends of enemies.
> And hitherto doth love on fortune tend;
> For who not needs shall never lack a friend,
> And who in want a hollow friend doth try
> Directly seasons him his enemy.
>
> *Hamlet*, III.2.

[A direct reflection on Bacon, who not only deserted Essex, understandably, but took a leading part in his prosecution at the trial, incurring much odium thereby. Dover Wilson perceptively saw the flecks of Essex in Hamlet, but not that the Succession to the throne was the overriding concern of the Queen's last years, 1600–3. As frequently Shakespeare's work at the time reflected this. The date is 1601.]

> Things small as nothing, for request's sake only,
> He makes important: possessed he is with greatness,
> And speaks not to himself but with a pride
> That quarrels at self-breath . . .
>
> *Troilus and Cressida*, ii.3.

[This had been precisely Essex's way with the Queen, and it ruined their relations. Shakespeare, from constant performances at Court, could observe from close at hand.]

> When Fortune in her shift and change of mood
> Spurns down her late beloved, all his dependants,
> Which laboured after him to the mountain's top
> Even on their knees and hands, let him fall down,
> Not one accompanying his declining foot.
>
> *Timon of Athens*, i.1.

[A later reflection on what precisely happened: Essex's followers went over to his opponent, Cecil.]

> Men shut their doors against a setting sun.
>
> *Timon of Athens*, i.2.

> The loyalty well held to fools does make
> Our faith mere folly. Yet he that can endure
> To follow with his allegiance a fallen lord
> Does conquer him that did his master conquer
> And earns a place in the story.
>
> *Antony and Cleopatra*, iii.13.

> Your lion, that holds his pole-axe sitting on a close-stool, will be
> given to Ajax.
>
> *Love's Labour's Lost*, v.2.

[Richard Field, Shakespeare's publisher from Stratford, published Harington's *Metamorphosis of Ajax*, i.e. a jakes, which he metamorphosed into a water-closet, in 1596. The revised and 'augmented' text of the play was published in 1598; this would have been one of the up-to-date additions. For Harington, a congenial personality, *v.* my *Eminent Elizabethans.*]

> Say his name, good friend.
> – Richard du Champ.

Cymbeline, iv.2.

[This is a complimentary allusion to Richard Field, appropriately in French; for Field had married Mrs Vautrollier, widow of the well-known French printer in Blackfriars. Field's list comprised a number of translations from French, as well as from Spanish.

Shakespeare's little joke is appropriate, for in Spanish Field called himself Ricardo del Campo. Actually, in 1594, he had published Antonio Pèrez' *Pedaços de historia, o relaçiones*, dedicated to Essex.

The more one goes into these associations in detail, with historical perception, the more one sees how they come together and corroborate each other.]

Tastes

ʒ

>   . . . a schoolmaster
> Well seen in music.

The Taming of the Shrew, i.2.

> Music to hear, why hear'st thou music sadly?
> Sweets with sweets war not, joy delights in joy:
> Why lov'st thou that which thou receiv'st not gladly,
> Or else receiv'st with pleasure thine annoy?
> If the true concord of well-tunèd sounds,
> By unions married, do offend thine ear,
> Thee do but sweetly chide thee who confounds
> In singleness the parts that thou shouldst bear.
> Mark how one string, sweet husband to another,
> Strikes each in each by mutual ordering.

Sonnet 8

[Addressed to the young Patron.]

>   . . . music oft hath such a charm
> To make bad good, and good provoke to harm.

Measure for Measure, iv.1.

[A reminiscence of the Dark Lady's musical charm?]

> Give me some music; music, moody food
> Of us that trade in love.

Antony and Cleopatra, ii.5.

> If music be the food of love, play on;
> Give me excess of it, that, surfeiting,

The appetite may sicken and so die.
That strain again! It had a dying fall:
O, it came o'er my ear like the sweet sound
That breathes upon a bank of violets,
Stealing and giving odour.

Twelfth Night, i.1.

How silver-sweet sound lovers' tongues by night,
Like softest music to attending ears.

Romeo and Juliet, ii.2.

Visit by night your lady's chamber window
With some sweet consort. To their instruments
Tune a deploring dump; the night's dead silence
Will well become such sweet-complaining grievance.

The Two Gentlemen of Verona, iii.2.

That old and antique song we heard last night –
Methought it did relieve my passion much,
More than light airs and recollected terms
Of these most brisk and giddy-pacèd times.

Twelfth Night, ii.4.

What music is this?
I do but partly know, sir – it is music in parts.
Know you the musicians? Who play they to?
To the hearers, sir.
At whose pleasure, friend?
At mine, sir, and theirs that love music.

Troilus and Cressida, iii.1.

How sour sweet music is
When time is broke and no proportion kept!
So it is in the music of men's lives.
And here have I the daintiness of ear
To check time broke in a disordered string –
But for the concord of my state and time
Had not an ear to hear my true time broke.

Richard II, v.5.

. . . They do no more adhere and keep place together than the
Hundredth Psalm to the tune of 'Greensleeves'.
The Merry Wives of Windsor, ii.1.

Let the sky rain potatoes, let it thunder to the tune of Greensleeves.
The Merry Wives of Windsor, v.5.

[Sweet potatoes were thought aphrodiasiac; 'Greensleeves' the most
popular of Elizabethan songs.]

I see what thou wert if 'Fortune thy Foe' were (not Nature) thy
friend.
The Merry Wives of Windsor, iii.3.

Best sing it to the tune of 'Light o' Love'.
– It is too heavy for so light a tune.
The Two Gentlemen of Verona, i.2.

Clap us into 'Light o' Love': that goes without a burden.
Much Ado About Nothing, iii.4.

[There are numerous references to popular songs, catches and ballads of
the time – besides the exquisite songs of which he wrote the words –
himself the most musical of all English dramatists.]

I am never merry when I hear sweet music . . .
The reason is, your spirits are attentive;
For, do but note a wild and wanton herd,
Or race of youthful and unhandled colts,
Fetching mad bounds, bellowing and neighing loud . . .
If they but hear perchance a trumpet sound,
Or any air of music touch their ears,
You shall perceive them make a mutual stand,
Their savage eyes turned to a modest gaze
By the sweet power of music. Therefore the poet
Did feign that Orpheus drew trees, stones, and floods –
Since nought so stockish, hard, and full of rage,
But music for the time doth change his nature.
The Merchant of Venice, v.1.

Orpheus with his lute made trees,
And the mountain tops that freeze,
    Bow themselves, when he did sing:
To his music plants and flowers
Ever sprung, as sun and showers
    There had made a lasting spring.

Every thing that heard him play,
Even the billows of the sea,
    Hung their heads, and then lay by.
In sweet music is such art,
Killing care and grief of heart
    Fall asleep, or hearing, die.

Henry VIII, iii.1.

Musicians! O, musicians – 'Heart's ease', 'Heart's ease'. O, an ye
will have me live, play 'Heart's ease'.
    Why 'Heart's ease'?
O, musicians, because my heart itself plays 'My heart is full of woe.'
O, play me some merry dump to comfort me . . .

    'When griping grief the heart doth wound,
        And doleful dumps the mind oppress,
    Then music with her silver sound – '[1]

Why 'silver sound'? Why 'music with her silver sound'? . . .
    Marry, sir, because silver hath a sweet sound.
Pretty! what say you?
    I say 'silver sound', because musicians sound for silver . . .
O, I cry you mercy. You are the singer – I will say for you: it is,
'music with her silver sound', because musicians have no gold for
sounding:

    'Then music with her silver sound
        With speedy help doth lend redress.'

Romeo and Juliet, iv.5.

Loud music is too harsh for ladies' heads
Since they love men in arms as well as beds.

Pericles, ii.3.

[1] Shakespeare is here making fun of an earlier song by Richard Edwards.

The fault will be in the music, if you be not wooed in good time . . .
There is measure in everything, and so dance out the answer . . .
Wooing, wedding, and repenting, is as a Scotch jig, a measure and a
cinquepace. The first suit is hot and hasty, like a Scotch jig, and full
as fantastical. The wedding, mannerly modest, as a measure, full of
state and ancientry. And then comes repentance and, with his bad
legs, falls into the cinquepace faster and faster, till he sink into his
grave.

Much Ado About Nothing, II.1.

I have neither the scholar's melancholy, which is emulation; nor the
musician's, which is fantastical.

As You Like It, IV.1.

The man that hath no music in himself,
Nor is not moved with concord of sweet sounds,
Is fit for treasons, stratagems, and spoils.
The motions of his spirit are dull as night,
And his affections dark as Erebus.
Let no such man be trusted.

The Merchant of Venice, V.1.

. . . he loves no plays
. . . he hears no music . . . seldom he smiles.
Such men as he are never at heart's ease . . .
And therefore are they very dangerous.

Julius Caesar, I.2.

While we do admire
This virtue and this moral discipline,
Let's be no stoics nor no stocks, I pray;
Or so devote to Aristotle's checks
As Ovid be an outcast quite abjured.
Balk logic with acquaintance that you have
And practise rhetoric in your common talk;
Music and poesy use to quicken you
The mathematics and the metaphysics,
Fall to them as your stomach serves you:
No profit grows where is no pleasure ta'en,
In brief, sir, study what you most affect.

The Taming of the Shrew, I.1.

When in the chronicle of wasted time
I see descriptions of the fairest wights,
And beauty making beautiful old rhyme
In praise of ladies dead and lovely knights . . .

                                                    Sonnet 106

[He was at this time reading Chaucer's 'Knight's Tale', which provided
some material for *A Midsummer Night's Dream*.]

Before these bastard signs of fair were born,
Or durst inhabit on a living brow:
Before the golden tresses of the dead,
The right of sepulchres, were shorn away
To live a second life on second head.

                                                    Sonnet 68

O, if in black my lady's brows be decked,
It mourns that painting and usurping hair
Should ravish doters with a false aspect.

                                    Love's Labour's Lost, iv.3.

So are those crispèd snaky locks
Which make such wanton gambols with the wind,
Upon supposèd fairness often known
To be the dowry of a second head –
The skull that bred them in the sepulchre.

                                    The Merchant of Venice, iii.2.

Yet black brows, they say,
Become some women best, so that there be not
Too much hair there, but in a semi-circle
Or a half-moon made with a pen.

                                    The Winter's Tale, ii.1.

I'll view the manners of the town,
Peruse the traders, gaze upon the buildings.

                                    The Comedy of Errors, i.2.

From our troops I strayed
To gaze upon a ruinous monastery.

                                    Titus Andronicus, v.1.

Bare ruined choirs, where late the sweet birds sang.

Sonnet 73

Tonight we'll wander through the streets, and note
The qualities of the people.

Antony and Cleopatra, i.1.

[John Aubrey corroborates this obvious taste: 'Ben Jonson and he did gather humours of men daily wherever they came.']

When we mean to build
We first survey the plot, then draw the model;
And when we see the figure of the house,
Then must we rate the cost of the erection.
Which, if we find outweighs ability,
What do we then but draw anew the model
In fewer offices, or at last desist
To build at all.

2 Henry IV, i.3.

[Shakespeare bought New Place in 1597, and next year was making repairs there. The play's date is 1598.]

First, her bedchamber: it was hanged
With tapestry of silk and silver: the story
Proud Cleopatra, when she met her Roman
And Cydnus swelled above the banks, or for
The press of boats or pride: a piece of work
So bravely done, so rich, that it did strive
In workmanship and value: which I wondered
Could be rarely and exactly wrought
Since the true life on it was –
                    . . . the chimney
Is south the chamber, and the chimney piece
Chaste Dian bathing. Never saw I figures
So likely to report themselves: the cutter
Was as another nature, dumb – outwent her,
Motion and breath left out . . .
                    The roof o' the chamber
With golden cherubins is fretted; her andirons –
I had forgot them – were two winking Cupids

Of silver, each on one foot standing, nicely
Depending on their brands.

Cymbeline, ii.4.

Carry him gently to my fairest chamber,
And hang it round with all my wanton pictures,
Balm his foul head in warm distillèd waters,
And burn sweet wood to make the lodging sweet . . .
Let one attend him with a silver basin,
Full of rose-water and bestrewed with flowers;
Another bear the ewer, the third a diaper,
And say, 'Will it please your lordship cool your hands?'
Someone be ready with a costly suit,
And ask him what apparel he will wear;
Another tell him of his hounds and horse.

The Taming of the Shrew, Induction, 1.

[This early play reflects the sophistication of his tastes with his entry into the Southampton circle.]

Dost thou love pictures? We will fetch thee straight
Adonis painted by a running brook,
And Cytherea all in sedges hid
Which seem to move and wanton with her breath,
Even as the waving sedges play with wind.
– We'll show thee Io as she was a maid,
And how she was beguilèd and surprised,
As lively painted as the deed was done.

The Taming of the Shrew, Induction, 2.

[Contemporary with his writing *Venus and Adonis*, 1593.]

Painter: You are rapt, sir, in some work, some dedication
To the great lord?
Poet: A thing slipped idly from me.
Our poesy is as a gum, which oozes
From whence 'tis nourished. The fire in the flint
Shows not till it be struck: our gentle flame
Provokes itself and, like the current, flies
Each bound it chafes. What have you there?
Painter: A picture, sir. Whence comes your book forth?

Poet: Upon the heels of my presentment [present], sir.
Let's see your piece.
Painter: 'Tis a good piece.
Poet: So 'tis. This comes off well and excellent.
Painter: Indifferent [moderately].
Poet: Admirable! How this grace
Speaks his own standing! What a mental power
This eye shoots forth! How big imagination
Moves in this lip! To the dumbness of the gesture
One might interpret.
Painter: It is a pretty mocking of the life.
Here is a touch. Is it good?
Poet: I'll say of it,
It tutors nature: artificial [artistic] strife
Lives in these touches livelier than life.

Timon of Athens, i.1.

[Jacobean patronage and art patter. 1609.]

A piece many years in doing, and now newly performed by that rare
Italian master, Julio Romano – who, had he himself eternity and
could put breath into his work, would beguile Nature of her custom,
so perfectly is he her ape.

The Winter's Tale, v.2.

[This has the interest of expressing contemporary aesthetic standards –
fidelity to nature.]

The painting is almost the natural man;
For since dishonour traffics with man's nature,
He is but outside; these pencilled figures are
Even such as they give out.

Timon of Athens, i.1.

Why should a man, whose blood is warm within,
Sit like his grandsire cut in alabaster?

The Merchant of Venice, i.1.

        Sore shaming
Those rich-left heirs that let their fathers lie
Without a monument.

Cymbeline, iv.2.

> ... but as a monument
> Thus in a chapel lying.
>
> *Cymbeline*, ii.2.

> like a taper in some monument
> Doth shine upon the dead man's earthy cheeks
>
> *Titus Andronicus*, ii.3.

> And on your family's old monument
> Hang mournful epitaphs.
>
> *Much Ado About Nothing*, iv.1.

> She sat like Patience on a monument.
>
> *Twelfth Night*, ii.4.

> Thou dost look
> Like Patience gazing on kings' graves.
>
> *Pericles*, v.1.

[Monuments and monumental sculpture were a particular feature of the age, and he seems to have taken particular notice of them.]

> In my youth I never did apply
> Hot and rebellious liquors in my blood,
> Nor did not with unbashful forehead woo
> The means of weakness and debility.
>
> *As You Like It*, ii.3.

What's a drunken man like, fool?
– Like a drowned man, a fool, and a madman: one draught above heat makes him a fool, the second mads him, and a third drowns him.

> *Twelfth Night*, i.5.

They say you are a melancholy fellow.
– I am so; I do love it better than laughing. Those that are in extremity of either are abominable fellows, and betray themselves to every modern censure [ordinary judgment] worse than drunkards.

> *As You Like It*, iv.1.

Antony: Strike the vessels, ho! Here is to Caesar!
Octavius Caesar:　　　　　　　　I could well forbear it.

It's a monstrous labour when I wash my brain,
And it grows fouler.
Antony: Be a child o'the time . . .
Caesar: But I had rather fast from all four days
Than drink so much in one.

Antony and Cleopatra, ii.7.

I am as melancholy as a gib [tom] cat, or a lugged bear.
– Or an old lion, or a lover's lute.
Yea, or the drone of a Lincolnshire bagpipe.
– What sayest thou to a hare, or the melancholy of Moorditch?

1 Henry IV, i.2.

O God, methinks it were a happy life
To be no better than a homely swain;
To sit upon a hill as I do now,
To carve out dials quaintly, point by point,
Thereby to see the minutes how they run,
How many make the hour full complete,
How many hours bring about the day,
How many days will finish up the year,
How many years a mortal man may live.
When this is known, then to divide the times:
So many hours must I tend my flock;
So many hours must I take my rest;
So many hours must I contemplate;
So many hours must I sport myself;
So many days my ewes have been with young;
So many weeks ere the poor fools will ean [give birth];
So many years ere I shall shear the fleece . . .
Gives not the hawthorn bush a sweeter shade
To shepherds, looking on their silly sheep,
Than doth a rich embroidered canopy
To kings, that fear their subjects' treachery . . .
And to conclude, the shepherd's homely curds,
His cold thin drink out of his leather bottle,
His wonted sleep under a fresh tree's shade –
All which secure and sweetly he enjoys.

3 Henry VI, ii.5.

I abhore such rackers of orthography as to speak 'dout' *sine* [without] b, when he should say 'doubt'; 'det' when he should pronounce 'debt' – d.e.b.t. He clepeth [calls] a calf 'cauf', half 'hauf'; neighbour 'nebour', neigh abbreviated 'ne'.

Love's Labour's Lost, v.1.

A sad tale's best for winter. I have one
Of sprites and goblins.

The Winter's Tale, ii.1.

The People

There have been many great men that have flattered the people, who ne'er loved them; and there be many that they have loved, they know not wherefore. So that if they love they know not why, they hate upon no better a ground.

Coriolanus, ii.1.

          Speak
To the people, not by your own instruction,
But with such words that are but rooted in
Your tongue, though but bastards and syllables
Of no allowance to your bosom's truth.
Now, this no more dishonours you at all
Than to take in a town with gentle words . . .
I would dissemble with my nature where
My fortunes and my friends at stake required
I should do so in honour.

Coriolanus, iii.2.

          Where gentry, title, wisdom
Cannot conclude but by the Yea and No
Of general ignorance, it must omit
Real necessities, and give way the while
To unstable slightness. Purpose so barred, it follows
Nothing is done to purpose . . .
The multitudinous tongue – let them not lick
The sweet which is their poison. Your dishonour
Mangles true judgment, and bereaves the state
Of that integrity which should become it –
Not having the power to do the good it would
For the ill which doth control it.

Coriolanus, iii.1.

147

And manhood is called foolery when it stands
Against a falling fabric.

Ibid.

Our slippery people,
Whose love is never linked to the deserver
Till his deserts are passed.

Antony and Cleopatra, I.2.

Look, as I blow this feather from my face,
And as the air blows it to me again,
Obeying with my wind when I do blow,
And yielding to another when it blows,
Commanded always by the greater gust –
Such is the lightness of you common men.

3 Henry VI, III.1.

Cinna: I am Cinna the poet, I am Cinna the poet.
Citizen: Tear him for his bad verses, tear him for his bad verses.
Cinna: I am not Cinna the conspirator.
Citizen: It is no matter, his name's Cinna. Pluck but his name out of his heart, and turn him going.
Citizens: Tear him, tear him! Come, brands, ho! firebrands! Burn all!

Julius Caesar, III.3.

Jack Cade: Now go some and pull down the Savoy. Others to the Inns of Court. Down with them all . . . Burn all the records of the realm . . . And henceforward all things shall be in common.

2 Henry VI, IV.6.

Jack Cade: Be it known unto thee by these presence [presents], even the presence of Lord Mortimer, that I am the besom [broom] that must sweep the Court clean of such filth as thou art. Thou hast most traitorously corrupted the youth of the realm in erecting a grammar-school. And whereas, before, our fathers had no other books but the score and the tally, thou hast caused printing to be used. And, contrary to the king, his crown and dignity, thou hast built a paper-mill. It will be proved to thy face that thou hast men about thee that usually talk of a noun and a verb, and such abominable words as no Christian ear can endure to hear.

2 Henry VI, IV.6.

[A parody of the form of an official proclamation; the rebel Jack Cade, claimed to be Lord Mortimer.]

> *Jack Cade:* And you, base peasants . . . will you needs be hanged
> with your pardons about your necks? . . . I thought ye would never
> have given out these arms till you had recovered your ancient
> freedom. But you are all recreants and dastards, and delight to live
> in slavery . . . Was ever feather so lightly blown to and fro as this
> multitude?
>
> > *2 Henry VI*, iv.8.

> An habitation giddy and unsure
> Hath he that buildeth on the vulgar heart.
>
> > *2 Henry IV*, i.3.

> *1st Servingman:* Let me have war, say I: it exceeds peace as far as day
> does night: it's sprightly, waking, audible, and full of vent. Peace is a
> very apoplexy, lethargy; mulled, deaf, sleepy, insensible; a getter of
> more bastard children than war's a destroyer of men.
> *2nd Servingman:* Tis so; and as war, in some sort, may be said to be a
> ravisher, so it cannot be denied but peace is a great maker of
> cuckolds.
> *1st Servingman:* Aye, and it makes men hate one another.
> *3rd Servingman:* Reason – because they then less need one another.
>
> > *Coriolanus*, iv.5.

[The play was written after the peace of 1604 ended the long war with Spain. In the background we have the Midlands disturbances of 1607–8, over the dearth and lack of grain. These spread to Warwickshire, where Shakespeare had become a landowner.]

> What authority surfeits on would relieve us. If they would yield
> us but the superfluity, while it was wholesome, we might guess they
> relieved us humanely . . . Care for us! They ne'er cared for us yet –
> suffer us to famish and their storehouses crammed with grain; make
> edicts for usury, to support usurers . . . and provide more piercing
> statutes daily to chain up and restrain the poor.
>
> > *Coriolanus*, i.1.

And that's the wavering commons; for their love
Lies in their purses, and who empties them
By so much fills their hearts with deadly hate.

Richard II, ii.2.

I trust I may not trust thee, for thy word
Is but the vain breath of a common man.

King John, iii.1.

Some Contemporary References

❧

'Tis since the earthquake now eleven years . . .
Sitting in the sun under the dovehouse wall . . .
'Shake', quoth the dovehouse. 'Twas no need I trow
To bid me trudge;
And since that time it is eleven years.

Romeo and Juliet, 1.3.

[This refers to the earthquake of 1583; the play's date is 1594.]

Other men . . .
Put forth their sons to seek preferment out:
Some to the wars, to try their fortune there;
Some to discover islands far away;
Some to the studious universities . . .
He cannot be a perfect man
Not being tried and tutored in the world:
Experience is by industry achieved.

The Two Gentlemen of Verona, 1.3.

[A crisp summing up of the age, the date of the play being 1592–3.]

One inch of delay more is a South Sea of discovery.

As You Like It, 111.2.

[The first English penetration into the Pacific, the South Sea – Drake's, followed by Cavendish's, then Richard Hawkins' – belonged to just these decades; the play's date is 1598.]

> . . . I should think of shallows and flats,
> And see my wealthy *Andrew* docked in sand,
> Vailing her high top lower than her ribs.
>
> *The Merchant of Venice*, I.1.

[At the capture of Cadiz, 1596, the galleon *St Andrew* was driven in upon the sand of the inner harbour.]

> . . . more lines than is in the new map with the augmentation of the Indies.
>
> *Twelfth Night*, III.2.

[Molyneux' map, criss-crossed by rhumb-lines, appeared in Hakluyt's *Principal Navigations*.]

> You are now sailed into the north of my lady's opinion, where you will hang like an icicle on a Dutchman's beard.
>
> *Ibid.*

[Refers to Barentz's recent Arctic voyage of 1596–7.]

> It cannot be sounded: it hath an unknown bottom like the bay of Portugal.
>
> *As You Like It*, IV.1.

> Her husband's to Aleppo gone, master o' the *Tiger*.
>
> *Macbeth*, I.3.

[The *Tiger* was a well-known armed merchantman engaged in the Levant trade, and in the news this year 1606.]

> As many lies as will lie in thy sheet of paper, although the sheet were big enough for the bed of Ware.
>
> *Twelfth Night*, III.2.

[This largest of Elizabethan beds happily survives in the Victoria and Albert Museum, South Kensington.]

> She is spherical, like a globe – I could find out countries in her.
> – In what part of her body stands Ireland?
> Marry, sir, in her buttocks: I found it out by the bogs.

– Where Scotland?

I found it out by the barrenness: hard in the palm of the hand.

– Where France?

In her forehead: armed and reverted, making war against her heir.[1]

– Where England?

I looked for the chalky cliffs, but I could find no whiteness in them. But I guess it stood in her chin, by the salt rheum that ran between France and it.

– Where Spain?

Faith, I saw not; but I felt it hot in her breath.

– Where America, the Indies?

O, sir, upon her nose, all o'er-embellished with rubies, carbuncles, sapphires, declining their rich aspect to the hot breath of Spain, who sent whole armadoes of carracks to be ballast at her nose.

– Where stood Belgia, the Netherlands?

O, sir, I did not look so low.

The Comedy of Errors, iii.2.

Report of fashions in proud Italy,
Whose manners still [ever] our tardy apish nation
Limps after in base imitation.

Richard II, ii.1.

How oddly he is suited! I think he bought his doublet in Italy, his round hose in France, his bonnet in Germany, and his behaviour everywhere.

The Merchant of Venice, i.3.

Farewell, Monsieur Traveller: look you lisp, and wear strange suits, disable all the benefits of your own country, be out of love with your nativity, and almost chide God for making you that countenance you are – or I will scarce think you have swum in a gondola.

As You Like It, iv.1.

This Armado is a Spaniard that keeps here in Court,
A phantasm, a Monarcho, and one that makes sport
To the Prince.

Love's Labour's Lost, iv.1.

[Another hit at Pèrez. Queen Elizabeth I had a dwarf named Monarcho.]

[1] Henry of Navarre succeeded as Henri IV in 1589, but was fought by the Catholic League until the surrender of Paris in 1594. The play's date is 1591–2.

> The uncivil kerns of Ireland are in arms
> And temper clay with blood of Englishmen:
> To Ireland will you lead a band of men,
> Collected choicely, from each county some,
> And try your hap against the Irishmen.
>
> *2 Henry VI*, iii.1.

[The Elizabethans were engaged in a prolonged struggle to reduce Ireland to civil order – hence the term 'uncivil' kerns, the light-armed soldiers of endemic Celtic warfare. In years of crisis government imposed a regular draft from each county, all down the west coast of England, for service in Ireland: 'from each county some'. Precisely.]

> We must supplant those rough, rug-headed kerns,
> Which live like venom where no venom else
> But only they have privilege to live.
>
> *Richard II*, ii.1.

['Rug-headed' refers to the glibs, hair worn over the eyes, forbidden by Statute, since it made disguise so easy.]

> Like a shag-haired crafty kern
> Hath he conversed with the enemy.
>
> *2 Henry VI*, iii.1.

> You rode like a kern of Ireland, your French hose off and in your strait strossers [breeks].
>
> *Henry V*, iii.7.

> The merciless Macdonald,
> Worthy to be a rebel . . .
> from the Western Isles
> Of kerns and gallowglasses is supplied.

[Gallowglasses were the more regular retainers of Celtic chieftains, in Gaelic Scotland as in Ireland – the Celtic fringe which the Renaissance state was engaged in reducing to order, *cf.* Wales and Brittany.]

> Justice had, with valour armed,
> Compelled these skipping kerns to trust their heels.
>
> *Macbeth*, i.2.

with a mighty power
Of gallowglasses and stout kerns
Is marching hitherward.

2 Henry VI, IV.9.

The lining of his coffers shall make coats
To deck our soldiers for these Irish wars.

Richard II, I.4.

[The government paid out 'coat and conduct' money for each soldier levied from western counties to serve in Ireland.]

Among the soldiers this is muttered,
That here you maintain several factions,
And whilst a field should be dispatched and fought
You are disputing of your generals.
One would have lingering wars with little cost,
Another would fly swift, but wanteth wings;
A third thinks, without expense at all,
By guileful fair words peace may be obtained.

1 Henry VI, I.1.

[A fair summing up of the situation, and of attitudes towards the war when the play was written, 1591 – considerable disputes as to who should command, while the Queen always favoured the third approach.]

That the star-gazers, having writ on death,
May say the plague is banished by thy breath.

Venus and Adonis

Why should the private pleasure of some one
Become the public plague of many moe?

The Rape of Lucrece

Thus pour the stars down plagues for perjury.

Love's Labour's Lost, V.2.

If heaven have any grievous plague in store.

Richard III, I.3.

[The years 1592 and 1593 were years of severe plague, which is much in the background – and many phrases refer to it in the works of these years, which include of course the Sonnets.]

> But when the planets
> In evil mixture to disorder wander,
> What plagues!
>
> *Troilus and Cressida*, I.3.

> Be as a planetary plague, when Jove
> Will o'er some high-viced city hang his poison
> In the sick air.
>
> *Timon of Athens*, IV.3.

> Even so quickly may one catch the plague.
>
> *Twelfth Night*, I.5.

> thy currish spirit
> Governed a wolf, who hanged for human slaughter . . .

> thy desires
> Are wolvish, bloody, starved and ravenous.
>
> *The Merchant of Venice*, IV.1.

[The case of Dr Lopez created a sensation in 1594, for, a Jew, he was accused of conspiring to poison the Queen for Spanish pay. He was an intelligence man, physician to the Queen, who did not believe him guilty. But Essex, whom he had offended, drove on the case, which released a disgraceful outburst of anti-Semitism. This led to a revival of Marlowe's *The Jew of Malta*: Shakespeare then went one better with *The Merchant of Venice*, in 1596. The Latin form of Lopez, *lupus* means a wolf: hence the reference.]

> The mortal moon hath her eclipse endured,
> And the sad augurs mock their own presage;
> Incertainties now crown themselves assured,
> And peace proclaims olives of endless age.
>
> Sonnet 107

[Queen Elizabeth emerged from the shadow of the Lopez conspiracy, with his execution *at the same time* as the peace in France with the surrender of Paris to Henri IV, i.e. early summer 1594.]

> . . . the fools of time,
> Which die for goodness who have lived for crime.
>
> *Sonnet 124*

[The persecution of Jesuits and seminary priests, 1594/5, who regarded themselves as martyrs for religion, where the normal view – with which Shakespeare aligned himself – was that they were enemies of the state, in wartime.]

> . . . in my travel's history:
> Wherein of antres [caves] and deserts idle,
> Rough quarries, rocks and hills whose heads touch heaven . . .
> And of the cannibals that each other eat,
> The Anthropophagi, and men whose heads
> Do grow beneath their shoulders.
>
> *Othello*, I.3.

[This reflects Ralegh's *Discourse on Guiana* of 1596.]

> Who would believe that there were mountaineers
> Dew-lapped like bulls, whose throats had hanging at them
> Wallets of flesh? Or that there were such men
> Whose heads stood in their breasts?
>
> *The Tempest*, III.3.

[This again reflects Shakespeare's reading of Ralegh and Hakluyt.]

> Thus Indian-like,
> Religious in mine error, I adore
> The sun that looks upon his worshipper.
>
> *All's Well That Ends Well*, I.3.

[This reflects Shakespeare's reading in the Voyages, in particular Hariot's *Brief and True Report of the Newfoundland of Virginia*.]

> Sometimes he is a kind of Puritan.
> – O, if I thought that, I'd beat him like a dog.
> What, for being a Puritan? . . .
> The devil a Puritan that he is, or anything constantly but a time-pleaser.
>
> *Twelfth Night*, II.3.

Though honesty be no Puritan ... it will wear the surplice of humility over the black gown of a big heart.

All's Well That Ends Well, I.3.

If men could be contented to be what they are, there were no fear in marriage; for young Charbon the Puritan and old Poysam the Papist – howsomever their heads are severed in religion – their heads are both one: they may jowl horns together like any deer in the herd.

All's Well That Ends Well, I.3.

Policy I hate; I'd as lief be a Brownist as a politician.

Twelfth Night, III.2.

['Politician' is almost a dirty word with Shakespeare, at least it carries a pejorative sense of factiousness and Machiavellian trickery, remote from our blameless specimens today. Browne, cleric and wife-beater, originated a religious faction of his own, Brownists or Congregationalists. He at least ultimately returned to the bosom of the Church.]

Am I politic? Am I subtle? Am I a Machiavel?

The Merry Wives of Windsor, III.1.

Than is the coal of fire upon the ice.

Coriolanus, I.1.

[The Thames was frozen over in the cold winter of 1607–8, when a fair was held upon it with fires burning. The play's date is 1608.]

The Garter Inn at Windsor

Bardolph: Sir, the Germans desire to have three of your horses: the Duke himself will be tomorrow at Court, and they are going to meet him.
Host: What Duke should that be comes so secretly? I hear not of him in the Court ...
They shall have my horses, but I'll make them pay. I'll sauce them: they have had my house a week at command. I have turned away my other guests: they must come off: I'll sauce them.

The Merry Wives of Windsor, IV.3.

Bardolph: Out, alas, sir! cozenage, mere cozenage.

Host: Where be my horses? Speak well of them, varletto.

Bardolph: Run away, with the cozeners. For, so soon as I came beyond Eton, they threw me off, from behind one of them, in a slough of mire. And set spurs and away, like three German devils, three Doctor Faustuses.

Host: They are gone but to meet the Duke, villain. Do not say they be fled: Germans are honest men . . .

Enter Sir Hugh Evans.

Evans: Have a care of your entertainments. There is a friend of mine come to town tells me there is three cozen-Germans that has cozened all the hosts of Readins, of Maidenhead, of Colebrook, of horses and money . . .

Enter Doctor Caius.

Caius: . . . it is tell-a me dat you make grand preparation for a Duke de Jarmany. By my trot, dere is no Duke dat de Court is know to come . . .

Host: Hue and Cry villain! . . . I am undone. Fly, run, Hue and Cry villain. I am undone.

The Merry Wives of Windsor, IV.5.

[Visit of German Count, later Duke of Württemberg, to Windsor.]

> They tax our policy, and call it cowardice,
> Count wisdom as no member of the war;
> Forestall prescience, and esteem no act
> But that of hand. The still and mental parts,
> That do contrive how many hands shall strike,
> When fitness calls them on, and know by measure
> Of their observant toil the enemies' weight –
> Why, this hath not a finger's dignity.
> They call this bed-work, mappery, closet-war.
> So that the ram that batters down the wall . . .
> They place before his hand that made the engine,
> Or those that with the fineness of their souls
> By reason guide his execution.

Troilus and Cressida, I.3.

[This precisely sums up the situation towards the end of the long war with Spain. The war party, the men of action – like Essex and Ralegh – were all for further blows against Spain, like the battering ram against

Cadiz. The government – the Queen and the Cecils – of 'the still and mental parts' were in favour of peace, on proper terms. As usual, Shakespeare's reason was on the side of government.But his personal affiliation had been with Southampton, his friends in opposition driving straight on the reefs to disaster in the Essex rising of 1601. Hence the bitterness of *Troilus and Cressida* – teeth on edge – of 1602: the subject of it disillusionment in both war and love, written for a special audience, not the populace, whose ignorant sympathies were always with Essex.]

> We go to gain a little patch of ground
> That hath in it no profit but the name . . .
> . . . I see
> The imminent death of twenty thousand men
> That, for a fantasy and trick of fame,
> Go to their graves like beds, fight for a plot
> Whereon the numbers cannot try the cause,
> Which is not tomb enough and continent
> To hide the slain.
>
> *Hamlet*, iv.4.

[The ding-dong struggle for Ostend 1600–1 involved immense numbers and innumerable casualties, disproportionately for a contracted area: its capture became a point of pride, of prestige at issue.]

> . . . Faith, here's an equivocator, that could swear in both the scales against either scale; who committed treason enough for God's sake, yet could not equivocate to heaven. O, come in, equivocator . . .
>
> Much drink may be said to be an equivocator with lechery. It makes him and it mars him; it sets him on, and it takes him off; it persuades him, and disheartens him; makes him stand to, and not stand to; in conclusion, equivocates him in a sleep, and, giving him the lie, leaves him . . .
>
> *Son:* What is a traitor?
> *Mother:* Why, one that swears and lies.
> *Son:* And be all traitors that do so?
> *Mother:* Every one that does so is a traitor and must be hanged.
>
> *Macbeth*, ii.3; iv.2.

[Gunpowder Plot, 1605. At the trial of Henry Garnet, the Jesuit Provincial, who had knowledge of a plot in confession but kept quiet about it, the Jesuit doctrine of equivocation on such a matter made the worst impression. Shakespeare shared the ordinary view of people on the subject.]

> *Master:* Good. Speak to the mariners. Fall to't yarely, or we run ourselves aground. Bestir, bestir!
> *Boatswain:* Heigh, my hearts! Cheerly, cheerly, my hearts! Yare, yare! Take in the topsail. Tend to the Master's whistle. Blow, till thou burst thy wind, if room enough! . . .
> [*A confused noise within.*] – 'Mercy on us.' 'We split, we split.' – 'Farewell, my wife and children.' 'Farewell, brother.' – 'We split, we split, we split.' 'Let's all sink with the King . . .'

> *Ariel:* I boarded the King's ship: now on the beak,
> Now in the waist, the deck, in every cabin,
> I flamed amazement. Sometime I'd divide
> And burn in many places. On the topmast,
> The yards, and bowsprit, would I flame distinctly,
> Then meet and join: Jove's lightnings, the precursors
> Of the dreadful thunderclaps, more momentary
> And sight-outrunning were not; the fire and cracks
> Of sulphurous roaring the most mighty Neptune
> Seem to besiege and make his bold waves tremble,
> Yea, his dread trident shake . . .
> *Prospero:* But are they, Ariel, safe?
> *Ariel:* Not a hair perished.
>
> *The Tempest*, I.1 and 2.

[The flagship of the Virginia voyage, 1609, the *Sea-Venture*, was wrecked in a hurricane and ran aground on Bermuda; the ship split, but not a life was lost, as in the play, which reflects every detail of the event, even the phenomenon of St Elmo's lightning, as in William Strachey's account sent home to Blackfriars, so familiar to Shakespeare.]

> the isle is full of noises,
> Sounds and sweet airs, that give delight and hurt not.
> Sometimes a thousand twangling instruments
> Will hum about mine ears; and sometimes voices
> That, if I then had waked after long sleep,
> Will make me sleep again.
>
> *The Tempest*, III.2.

[Bermuda, which the Elizabethans believed to be enchanted.]

Timon, digging: Gold! yellow, glittering, precious gold! No gods,
I am no idle votarist. Roots, you clear heavens!
Thus much of this will make black white, foul fair,
Wrong right, base noble, old young, coward valiant.
Ha, you gods, why this? What this, you gods? Why this
Will lug your priests and servants from your sides;
Pluck stout men's pillows from below their head.
This yellow slave
Will knit and break religions; bless the accursed;
Make the hoar leprosy adored; place thieves,
And give them title, knee and approbation,
With senators on the bench; this is it
That makes the wappered widow wed again . . .
                    Come, damnèd earth
Thou common whore of mankind, that put'st odds
Among the rout of nations . . .
Alcibiades: Here is some gold for thee.
Timon: Keep it: I cannot eat it . . .
Put up thy gold: go on. Here's gold: go on . . .
Alcibiades: Hast thou gold yet? I'll take the gold thou giv'st me.
Phrynia: ⎫
Timandra: ⎬ Give us some gold, good Timon. Hast thou more? . . .
. . . Well, more gold. What then?
Believe't, that we'll do anything for gold.

                              Timon of Athens, iv.3.

[This reflects the report that came back from the Jamestown colony,
1607, that the colonists were afflicted with a mania for digging for gold,
neglecting to plant.]

Characteristic Reflections

ะ

When I consider every thing that grows
Holds in perfection but a little moment,
That this huge stage presenteth nought but shows
Whereon the stars in secret influence comment;
When I perceive that men as plants increase,
Cheered and checked even by the self-same sky,
Vaunt in their youthful sap, at height decrease,
And wear their brave state out of memory . . .

Sonnet 15

Not marble, nor the gilded monuments
Of princes, shall outlive this powerful rhyme;
But you shall shine more bright in these contents
Than unswept stone, besmeared with sluttish time.
When wasteful war shall statues overturn,
And broils root out the work of masonry,
Nor Mars's sword nor war's quick fire shall burn
The living record of your memory.

Sonnet 55

The poor world is almost six thousand years old.

As You Like It, iv.1.

When I have seen by Time's fell hand defaced
The rich, proud cost of outworn buried age;
When sometime lofty towers I see down-razed,
And brass eternal slave to mortal rage . . .

Sonnet 64

For time is like a fashionable host,
That slightly shakes his parting guest by the hand
And, with his arms outstretched as he would fly,
Grasps in the comer. The welcome ever smiles,
And farewell goes out sighing.

Troilus and Cressida, iii.3.

Tired with all these, for restful death I cry,
As, to behold desert a beggar born,
And needy nothing trimmed in jollity,
And purest faith unhappily forsworn,
And gilded honour shamefully misplaced;
And maiden virtue rudely strumpeted,
And right perfection wrongfully disgraced;
And strength by limping sway disabled,
And art made tongue-tied by authority,
And folly, doctor-like, controlling skill,
And simple truth miscalled simplicity,
And captive good attending captain ill.

Sonnet 66

[The last line is an adaptation of a line of Marlowe's.]

Some glory in their birth, some in their skill,
Some in their wealth, some in their bodies' force;
Some in their garments, though new-fangled ill,
Some in their hawks and hounds, some in their horse.
And every humour hath his adjunct pleasure,
Wherein it finds a joy above the rest.

Sonnet 91

They that have power to hurt and will do none,
That do not do the thing they most do show,
Who, moving others, are themselves as stone,
Unmovèd, cold, and to temptation slow:
They rightly do inherit heaven's graces
And husband nature's riches from expense:
They are the lords and owners of their faces,
Others but stewards of their excellence.

Sonnet 94

> All things that are
> Are with more spirit chasèd than enjoyed.
>
> *The Merchant of Venice*, ii.6.

I have neither the scholar's melancholy, which is emulation; nor the musician's, which is fantastical; nor the courtier's, which is proud; nor the soldier's, which is ambitious; nor the lawyer's, which is politic; nor the lady's, which is nice [refined]; nor the lover's, which is all these.

> *As You Like It*, iv.1.

> A woman, that is like a German clock,
> Still a-repairing, ever out of frame,
> And never going aright, being a watch,
> But being watched that it might still go right.
>
> *Love's Labour's Lost*, iii.2.

> [Men's] fancies are more giddy and unfirm,
> More longing, wavering, sooner lost and worn
> Than women's are.
>
> *Twelfth Night*, .i.4.

> Thy husband is thy lord, thy life, thy keeper,
> Thy head, thy sovereign: one that cares for thee,
> And for thy maintenance commits his body
> To painful labour both by sea and land,
> To watch the night in storms, the day in cold,
> Whilst thou liest warm at home, secure and safe;
> And craves no other tribute at thy hands
> But love, fair looks, and true obedience.
>
> *The Taming of the Shrew*, v.2.

[This was the regular Elizabethan attitude on the subject – compare the marriage service in the old *Book of Common Prayer* to which Shakespeare, always a conformist, conformed. It needs no anachronistic comment with no sense of the time.]

> Reason, my son,
> Should choose himself a wife; but as good reason
> The father – all whose joy is nothing else
> But fair posterity – should hold some counsel
> In such a business.
>
> *The Winter's Tale*, iv.3.

If ever you have looked on better days,
If ever been where bells have knolled to church,
If ever sat at any goodman's feast,
If ever from your eyelids wiped a tear
And know what 'tis to pity and be pitied –
Let gentleness my strong enforcement be.

As You Like It, ii.7.

O good old man! how well in thee appears
The constant service of the antique world,
When service sweat for duty, not for meed [reward].
Thou art not for the fashion of these times,
Where none will sweat but for promotiòn
And, having that, do choke their service up
Even with the having.

As You Like It, ii.3.

Blow, blow, thou winter wind,
Thou art not so unkind
    As man's ingratitude . . .
Freeze, freeze, thou winter sky,
That dost not bite so nigh
    As benefits forgot;
Though thou the waters warp
Thy sting is not so sharp
    As friend remembered not.

As You Like It, ii.7.

I hate ingratitude more in a man
Than lying, vainness, babbling drunkenness,
Or any taint of vice whose strong corruption
Inhabits our frail blood.

Twelfth Night, iii.4.

Time hath . . . a wallet at his back,
Wherein he puts alms for oblivion,
A great-sized monster of ingratitudes.
Those scraps are good deeds past, which are devoured
As fast as they are made, forgot as soon
As done.

Troilus and Cressida, iii.3.

This fortress built by Nature for herself
Against infection and the hand of war,
This happy breed of men, this little world,
This precious stone set in the silver sea,
Which serves it in the office of a wall,
Or as a moat defensive to a house,
Against the envy of less happier lands –
This blessed plot, this earth, this realm, this England.

Richard II, II.1.

[This was written in the early 1590s, a few years after the defeat of the Armada of 1588.]

Our countrymen
Are men more ordered than when Julius Caesar
Smiled at their lack of skill, but found their courage
Worthy his frowning at; their discipline,
Now winged, with their courage will make known
To their approvers they are people such
That mend upon the world.

Cymbeline, II.4.

Not all the water in the rough rude sea
Can wash the balm from an anointed king.

Richard II, III.2.

Princes have but their titles for their glories,
An outward honour for an inward toil;
And for unfelt imaginatiòns
They often feel a world of restless cares.
So that between their titles and low name
There's nothing differs but the outward fame.

Richard III, I.4.

What infinite heart's ease
Must kings neglect that private men enjoy!
And what have kings that privates have not too
Save ceremony, save general ceremony?
And what art thou, thou idle ceremony?
What kind of god art thou that suffer'st more
Of mortal griefs than do thy worshippers?

What are thy rents? What are thy comings in?
O ceremony, show me but thy worth,
What is thy soul of adoratiòn?
Art thou aught else but place, degree, and form,
Creating awe and fear in other men? . . .

No, not all these thrice-gorgeous ceremony . . .
Can sleep so soundly as the wretched slave,
Who with a body filled and vacant mind,
Gets him to rest, crammed with distressful bread;
Never sees horrid night, the child of hell,
But, like a lackey, from the rise to set
Sweats in the eye of Phoebus, and all night
Sleeps in Elysium. Next day after dawn
Doth rise and help Hyperion to his horse,
And follows so the ever-running year
With profitable labour to his grave.
And, but for ceremony, such a wretch,
Winding up days with toil and nights with sleep,
Had the forehand and vantage of a king.
The slave, the member of the country's peace,
Enjoys it, but in gross brain little wots
What watch the king keeps to maintain the peace,
Whose hours the peasant best advantages.

Henry V, iv.1.

There is a mystery – with whom relation
Durst never meddle – in the soul of state,
Which hath an operation more divine
Than breath or pen can give expressure to.

Troilus and Cressida, iii.3.

The heavens themselves, the planets, and this centre
Observe degree, priority, and place,
Insisture, course, proportion, season, form,
Office, and custom, all in line of order . . .
            . . . O, when degree is shaked,
Which is the ladder to all high designs,
The enterprise is sick. How could communities,
Degrees in schools, and brotherhoods in cities,
Peaceful commerce from dividable shores,
The primogenitive and due of birth,

Prerogative of age, crowns, sceptres, laurels,
But by degree, stand in authentic place?
Take but degree away, untune that string,
And, hark what discord follows. Each thing meets
In mere oppugnancy . . .
Strength should be lord of imbecility [weakness].
Force should be right; or rather right and wrong . . .
Should lose their names, and so should justice too.
Then everything includes itself in power,
Power into will, will into appetite.
And appetite, a universal wolf,
Must make perforce a universal prey
And last eat up himself.

Troilus and Cressida, 1.3.

[This famous passage needs no extended comment, except to point out
that it is what Shakespeare enforced in all his plays from the beginning to
the end of his career: the absolute necessity of maintaining social order,
of observing degree according to function if society is to function, the
appalling consequences to humanity in undermining and overthrowing
it. Twentieth-century revolutions have borne out the insight of the writer
who of all had the greatest insight into human nature. Nor does it need
stressing that revolutions, whether French, German or Russian, whether
Communist, Nazi or Fascist, resolve into mere pursuit of power and eat
up their own offspring.]

Gonzalo: In the commonwealth I would by contraries
Execute all things. For no kind of traffic
Would I admit: no name of magistrate;
Letters should not be known; riches, poverty,
And use of service none; contract, succession,
Bourn, bound of land, tilth, vineyard, none;
No use of metal, corn, or wine, or oil;
No occupation; all men idle, all;
And women too, but innocent and pure;
No sovereignty . . .
All things in common nature should produce
Without sweat or endeavour. Treason, felony,
Sword, pike, knife, gun, or need of any engine,
Would I not have. But nature should bring forth,
Of its own kind, all foison [harvest], all abundance,

To feed my innocent people.
Sebastian: No marrying among his subjects?
Antonio: None, man: all idle – whores and knaves.
Gonzalo: I would with such perfection govern, sir,
To excel the golden age.

The Tempest, ii.1.

[This reflects Montaigne's account of primitive Communism: we see
what Shakespeare thought of it.]

The age is grown so picked [touchy] that the toe of the peasant
comes so near the heel of the courtier, he galls his kibe [chilblain].

Hamlet, v.1.

There is a tide in the affairs of men
Which, taken at the flood, leads on to fortune . . .
And we must take the current when it serves.

Julius Caesar, iv.3.

O world! thy slippery turns. Friends now fast sworn,
Whose double bosoms seem to wear one heart,
Whose hours, whose bed, whose meal, and exercise
Are still together, who twin, as 'twere, in love
Unseparable, shall within this hour,
On a dissension of a doit, break out
To bitterest enmity. So, fellest foes,
Whose passions and whose plots have broke their sleep
To take the one the other, by some chance,
By some trick not worth an egg, shall grow dear friends
And interjoin their issues.

Coriolanus, iv.4.

The loyalty well held to fools does make
Our faith mere folly.

Antony and Cleopatra, iii.3.

For men, like butterflies,
Show not their mealy wings but to the summer;
And not a man, for being simply man,
Hath any honour, but honour for those honours
That are without him, as places, riches, and favour,
Prizes of accident as oft as merit.

Troilus and Cressida, iii.3.

It hath been taught us from the primal state
That he which is was wished until he were,
And the ebbed man, ne'er loved till ne'er worth love,
Comes deared by being lacked.

Antony and Cleopatra, i.4.

A man may see how this world goes with no eyes. Look with thine
ears: see how yon justice rails upon yon simple thief . . . Change
places and, handy-dandy, which is the justice, which is the thief?
Thou has seen a farmer's dog bark at a beggar? And the creature
run from the cur?
   There thou mightst behold the great image of authority: a dog's
obeyed in office.
Thou rascal beadle, hold thy bloody hand!
Why dost thou lash that whore? Strip thine own back:
Thou hotly lust'st to use her in that kind
For which thou whipp'st her . . .
Robes and furred gowns hide all.

King Lear, iv.6.

   Get thee glass eyes,
And, like a scurvy politician, seem
To see the things thou dost not.

Ibid.

That smooth-faced gentleman, tickling Commodity,[1]
Commodity, the bias of the world;
The world, who of itself is peizèd [poised] well,
Made to run even upon even ground,
Till this advantage, this vile-drawing bias,
This sway of motion, this Commodity,
Makes it take head from all indifferency [impartiality],
From all direction, purpose, course, intent . . .
Well, while I am a beggar, I will rail
And say there is no sin but to be rich;
And being rich, my virtue then shall be
To say there is no vice but beggary.
Since kings break faith upon Commodity.

King John, ii.1.

[1] i.e. convenience, or expediency, especially political – self-interest.

They well deserve to have
That know the surest way to get.

Richard II, iii.3.

Honour pricks me on. Yea, but how if honour pricks me off when I
come on? How then? Can honour set to a leg? No. Or an arm? No.
Or take away the grief of a wound? No. Honour hath no skill in
surgery then? No. What is honour? A word. What is that word
honour? Air. A trim reckoning! Who hath it? He that died
o'Wednesday. Doth he feel it? No. Doth he hear it? No. It is
insensible then? Yea, to the dead. But it will not live with the living?
No. Why? Detraction will not suffer it. Therefore I'll none of it.
Honour is a mere scutcheon.

1 Henry IV, v.1.

The better part of valour is discretion.

1 Henry IV, v.4.

His valour cannot carry his discretion.
– His discretion, I am sure, cannot carry his valour.

A Midsummer Night's Dream, v.1.

O God, that men should put an enemy
In their mouths to steal away their brains.

Othello, ii.3.

Pleasure will be paid, one time or another.

Twelfth Night, ii.4.

Men shall deal unadvisedly sometimes
Which after-hours give leisure to repent.

Richard III, iv.4.

Heaven doth with us as we with torches do,
Not light them for themselves; for if our virtues
Did not go forth of us, 'twere all alike
As if we had them not.

Measure for Measure, i.1.

'Tis good for men to love their present pains
Upon example: so the spirit is eased;

And when the mind is quickened, out of doubt
The organs, though defunct and dead before,
Break up their drowsy grave and newly move
With casted slough and fresh legerity.

Henry V, IV.1.

When we our betters see bearing our woes,
We scarcely think our miseries our foes.
Who alone suffers, suffers most in the mind . . .
But then the mind doth much sufferance o'erskip
When grief hath mates, and bearing fellowship.

King Lear, III.6.

no man is the lord of anything –
Though in and of him there be much consisting –
Till he communicate his parts to others;
Nor doth he of himself know them for aught
Till he behold them formed in the applause
Where they're extended.

Troilus and Cressida, III.3.

One touch of nature makes the whole world kin.

Ibid.

Have more than thou showest,
Speak less than thou knowest,
Lend less than thou owest,
Ride more than thou goest [walk],
Learn more than thou trowest [know]
Set [stake] less than thou throwest . . .
Leave thy drink and thy whore,
And keep [live] in-a-door [within doors].
And thou shalt have more
Than two tens to a score.

King Lear, I.4.

There's no art
To find the mind's construction in the face.

Macbeth, I.4.

There is no vice so simple but assumes
Some mark of virtue on his outward parts.

The Merchant of Venice, III.2.

He that but fears the thing he would not know
Has by instinct knowledge from others' eyes
That what he feared is chanced.

2 Henry IV, i.1.

Use every man after his own desert, and who should 'scape whipping?

Hamlet, ii.2.

A dog's obeyed in office.

King Lear, iv.6.

O, it is excellent
To have a giant's strength, but it is tyrannous
To use it like a giant.

Measure for Measure, ii.2.

But man, proud man,
Dressed in a little brief authority,
Most ignorant of what he's most assured . . .
Plays such fantastic tricks before high heaven
As make the angels weep.

Ibid.

Authority, though it err like others,
Hath yet a kind of medicine in itself.

Ibid.

Thou hast nor youth nor age,
But as it were an after-dinner's sleep
Dreaming on both.

Measure for Measure, iii.1.

A jest's prosperity lies in the ear
Of him that hears it, never in the tongue
Of him that makes it.

Love's Labour's Lost, v.2.

Good name in man and woman . . .
Is the immediate jewel of their souls.

Othello, iii.3.

O, beware of jealousy:
It is the green-eyed monster that doth mock
The meat it feeds on; that cuckold lives in bliss
Who, certain of his fate, loves not his wronger;
But O, what damnèd minutes tells he o'er
Who dotes, yet doubts; suspects, yet soundly loves!

Ibid.

Jealous souls . . .
              are not ever jealous for the cause,
But jealous for they're jealous. It is a monster
Begot upon itself, born of itself.

Othello, III.4.

'Tis slander
Whose edge is sharper than the sword, whose tongue
Outvenoms all the worms of Nile, whose breath
Rides on the posting winds and doth belie
All corners of the world. Kings, queens and states,
Maids, matrons, nay, the secrets of the grave
This viperous slander enters.

Cymbeline, III.4.

The quality of mercy is not strained,
It droppeth as the gentle rain from heaven
Upon the place beneath. It is twice blessed:
It blesseth him that gives and him that takes.
'Tis mightiest in the mightiest: it becomes
The thronèd monarch better than his crown;
The sceptre shows the force of temporal power,
The attribute to awe and majesty,
Wherein doth sit the dread and fear of kings –
But mercy is above this sceptred sway,
It is enthronèd in the hearts of kings,
It is an attribute to God himself,
And earthly power doth then show likest God's
When mercy seasons justice.

The Merchant of Venice, IV.1.

No ceremony that to great ones 'longs,
Not the king's crown, nor the deputed sword,

The marshal's truncheon, nor the judge's robe,
Become them with one half so good a grace,
As mercy does.

Measure for Measure, II.2.

They say miracles are past, and we have our philosophical persons
to make modern [ordinary] and familiar things supernatural and
causeless. Hence is it that we make trifles of terrors, ensconcing
ourselves into seeming knowledge, when we should submit ourselves to an unknown fear.

All's Well That Ends Well, II.3.

In religion
What damnèd error but some sober brow
Will bless it and approve it with a text?

The Merchant of Venice, III.2.

Your 'if' is the only peacemaker. Much virtue in 'if'.

As You Like It, V.4.

O place, O form!
How often dost thou with thy case, thy habit,
Wrench awe from fools, and tie the wiser souls
To thy false seeming.

Measure for Measure, II.4.

O place and greatness! Millions of false eyes
Are stuck upon thee: volumes of report
Run with these false and most contrarious quests
Upon thy doings; thousand escapes of wit
Make thee the father of their idle dream,
And rack thee in their fancies!

Measure for Measure, IV.1.

No might nor greatness in mortality
Can censure 'scape: back-wounding calumny
The whitest virtue strikes. What king so strong
Can tie the gall up in the slanderous tongue?

Measure for Measure, III.2.

What great ones do the less will prattle of.

Twelfth Night, I.2.

The rarer action is
In virtue than in vengeance.

The Tempest, v.1.

From lowest place when virtuous things proceed,
The place is dignified by the doer's deed.
Where great additions swell us, and virtue none,
It is a dropsied honour . . .
The property by what it is should go
Not by the title . . .
Honours thrive
When rather from our acts we them derive
Than our foregoers. The mere word's a slave,
Debauched on every tomb, on every grave
A lying trophy, and as oft is dumb
Where dust and damned oblivion is the tomb
Of honoured bones indeed.

All's Well That Ends Well, ii.3.

Our remedies oft in ourselves do lie
Which we ascribe to heaven. The fated sky
Gives us free scope, only doth backward pull
Our slow designs when we ourselves are dull.

All's Well That Ends Well, i.1.

We, ignorant of ourselves,
Beg often our own harms, which the wise powers
Deny us for our good: so find we profit
By losing of our prayers.

Antony and Cleopatra, ii.1.

Full oft 'tis seen
Our means secure us, and our mere defects
Prove our commodities.

King Lear, iv.1.

There is some soul of goodness in things evil
Would men observingly distil it out . . .
Thus may we gather honey from the weed.

Henry V, iv.1.

. . . In this earthly world, where to do harm
Is often laudable, to do good sometime
Accounted dangerous folly.   *Macbeth*, iv.2.

It is the stars,
The stars above us govern our conditions.
Else one self mate and make could not beget
Such different issues.   *King Lear*, iv.3.

Few men rightly temper with the stars.   *3 Henry VI*, iv.6.

When remedies are past the griefs are ended
By seeing the worst, which late on hopes depended:
To mourn a mischief that is past and gone
Is the next way to draw new mischief on.
                                              Othello, i.3.

       . . . The worst is not
So long as we can say 'This is the worst.'
                                              King Lear, iv.1.

          To be worst,
The lowest and most dejected thing of fortune,
Stands still in esperance, lives not in fear:
The lamentable change is from the best.
                                              Ibid.

How poor are they that have not patience!
What wound did ever heal but by degrees?
                                              Othello, ii.3.

Ay, but to die, and go we know not where;
To lie in cold obstruction and to rot;
This sensible warm motion to become
A kneaded clod; and the delighted spirit
To bathe in fiery floods, or to reside
In thrilling region of thick-ribbed ice:
To be imprisoned in the viewless winds,

And blown with restless violence round about
The pendent world! Or to be worse than worst
Of those that lawless and incertain thoughts
Imagine howling: 'tis too horrible!
The weariest and most loathèd worldly life
That age, ache, penury and imprisonment
Can lay on nature is a paradise
To what we fear of death.

Measure for Measure, iii.1.

Reason thus with life:
If I do lose thee, I do lose a thing
That none but fools would keep: a breath thou art,
Servile to all the skyey influences,
That dost this habitation where thou keep'st
Hourly afflict.

Ibid.

Of all the wonders that I yet have heard
It seems to me most strange that men should fear,
Seeing that death, a necessary end,
Will come when it will come.

Julius Caesar, ii.2.

Men must endure
Their going hence even as their coming hither:
Ripeness is all.

King Lear, v.2.

He that of greatest works is finisher
Oft does them by the weakest minister.
Oft expectation fails, and most oft there
Where most it promises; and oft it hits
Where hope is coldest and despair most fits.

All's Well That Ends Well, ii.1.

'Tis not so above:
There is no shuffling, there the action lies
In his true nature; and we ourselves compelled
Even to the teeth and forehead of our faults
To give in evidence.

Hamlet, iii.3.

It is not so with Him that all things knows
As 'tis with us that square our guess by shows;
But most it is presumption in us when
The help of heaven we count the act of men.

All's Well That Ends Well, ii.1.

Why, all the souls that were were forfeit once,
And He that might the vantage best have took
Found out the remedy. How would you be
If He, which is the top of judgment, should
But judge you as you are? O, think on that!

Measure for Measure, ii.2.

Shakespeare's Will

‏❦

[Shakespeare's will is a characteristic Elizabethan will, drawn up in legal form by his lawyer, Francis Collins of Warwick. As with most wills it is intimately revealing of the man and of his circumstances at time of death. There are several points of interest. First, he dies a conforming Protestant; Elizabethan Catholic wills began with a different formula, willing one's soul to the mediation of the Blessed Virgin and 'all the holy company of heaven' – charming, but different.

Very much a family man, he is mainly concerned with providing for the succession of his immediate family to his property. Several paragraphs constitute a kind of trust for his second daughter Judith, every contingency provided for in lawyerly language. The bulk of his property went to his elder daughter Susanna and her husband, Dr John Hall, with succession to their only child, Elizabeth, who married (1) Thomas Nash, (2) Sir John Barnard. She, however, had no children, and Judith's died childless. The specific reservation of the next to the best bed in the house with its furniture to his widow testifies to Shakespeare's considerateness, for naturally the big best bed would be needed for the married couple, Susanna and her husband.

The number of bequests to Stratford townsmen shows his neighbourliness; we observe the careful social discrimination between esquire and gentleman, Shakespeare himself a gentleman, regularly referred to respectfully as 'Master' Shakespeare, a superior status for an actor. Most revealing are his bequests for rings to remember him by to the three leading fellows of his Company, formerly the Lord Chamberlain's, then the King's Men. And there is the reference to his tenement in Blackfriars, convenient to the theatre of which he was part-owner.

Markedly faithful to his native town, where he had rehabilitated the family's standing by buying the best house in the town and a good holding of property in and around, sufficient to maintain the status of an independent country gentleman, his will completely confirms the picture of the Stratford man who went to London to make a modest fortune in the theatre, and came back home to die.

All corroborated of course by Ben Jonson in the biographical tribute, prefaced to the First Folio, to the 'sweet swan of Avon' who made his flights

> upon the Thames,
> That so did take Eliza and our James.

As early as 1605 a pamphlet, *Ratsy's Ghost*, pointed enviously at his prospering; a reference to *Hamlet* makes clear who is in mind. 'Get thee to London . . . for there thou shalt learn to be frugal, for players were never so thrifty as they are now about London . . . to make thy hand a stranger to thy pocket, thy heart slow to perform thy tongue's promise. And when thou feelest thy purse well lined, buy thee some place or lordship in the country, that, growing weary of playing, thy money may there bring thee to dignity and reputation . . . Sir, I thank you, quoth the Player, for this good counsel. I promise you I will make use of it. For I have heard indeed of some that have gone to London very meanly and have come in time to be exceedingly wealthy.'

Shakespeare's fortune was sufficient to make him an independent gentleman, in his last years independent of playing or indeed of writing any more plays.]

25 March 1616

In the name of God, Amen. I, William Shakespeare, of Stratford upon Avon in the county of Warwick, gentleman, in perfect health and memory, God be praised, do make and ordain this my last will and testament in manner and form following.

That is to say, first I commend my soul into the hands of God my Creator, hoping and assuredly believing, through the only merits of Jesus Christ my Saviour, to be made partaker of life everlasting. And my body to the earth whereof it is made.

Item, I give and bequeath unto my daughter Judith £150 of lawful English money, to be paid unto her in manner and form following. That is to say, £100 in discharge of her marriage portion within one year after my decease – with consideration after the rate of 2 shillings in the £ for so long time as the same shall be unpaid to her after my decease. And the £50 residue thereof upon her surrendering of, or giving of such sufficient security as the overseers of this my will shall like of to surrender or grant, all her estate and right that shall descend or come unto her after my decease, or that she now hath of, in or to one copyhold tenement with the appurtenances lying and being in Stratford upon Avon aforesaid in the said county of Warwick, being parcel or holden of the manor of Rowington, unto my daughter Susanna Hall and her heirs for ever.

Item, I give and bequeath unto my said daughter Judith £150 more if she or any issue of her body be living at the end of three years next ensuing the day of the date of this my will – during which time my executors to pay her consideration from my decease according to the rate aforesaid. And if she die within the said term without issue of her body, then my will is and I do give and bequeath £100 thereof to my niece [i.e. grandchild]* Elizabeth Hall; and the £50 to be set forth by my executors during the life of my sister, Joan Hart, and the use and profit thereof coming shall be paid to my said sister Joan. And after her decease the said £50 shall remain amongst the children of my said sister, equally to be divided amongst them.

But if my said daughter Judith be living at the end of the said three years, or any issue of her body, then my will is and so I devise and bequeath the said £150 to be set out by my executors and overseers for the best benefit of her and her issue; and the stock not to be paid unto her so long as she shall be married and covert barren [childless]. But my will is that she shall have the consideration yearly paid unto her during her life, and after her decease the said stock and consideration to be paid to her children if she have any – and if not, to her executors or assigns, she living the said term after my decease. Provided that, if such husband as she, at the end of the said three years, be married unto or attain after, do sufficiently assure unto her and the issue of her body lands answerable to the portion by this my will given unto her – and to be adjudged so by my executors and overseers – then my will is that the said £150 shall be paid to such husband as shall make such assurance to his own use.

Item, I give and bequeath unto my said sister Joan £20 and all my wearing apparel, to be paid and delivered within one year after my decease. And I do will and devise unto her the house with the appurtenances in Stratford wherein she dwelleth for her natural life, under the yearly rent of 12d. Item, I give and bequeath unto her

---

* Elizabethans used the words 'niece' and 'cousin' more widely than we do, also using 'cousin' for nephew. In *The Contemporary Shakespeare* I regularise to modern usage.

three sons, William Hart, — Hart, and Michael Hart, £5 apiece to be paid within one year after my decease.

Item, I give and bequeath unto the said Elizabeth Hall all my plate (except my broad silver and gilt bowl) that I now have at the date of this my will.

Item, I give and bequeath unto the poor of Stratford aforesaid £10. To Mr Thomas Combe my sword; to Thomas Russell, esquire, £5; and to Francis Collins of the borough of Warwick in the county of Warwick, gentleman, £13.6.8. to be paid within one year after my decease. Item, I give and bequeath to Hamnet Sadler 26s 8d to buy him a ring; to William Reynolds, gentleman, 26s 8d to buy him a ring; to my godson William Walker 20s in gold; to Anthony Nash, gentleman, 26s 8d; and to my fellows, John Heming, Richard Burbage, and Henry Condell 26s 8d apiece to buy them rings.

Item, I give, will, bequeath and devise unto my daughter Susanna Hall, for better enabling of her to perform this my will and towards the performance thereof, all that capital messuage or tenement with the appurtenances in Stratford aforesaid called the New Place, wherein I now dwell. And two messuages or tenements with the appurtenances situate, lying and being in Henley Street within the borough of Stratford aforesaid. And all my barns, stables, orchards, gardens, lands, tenements and hereditaments whatsoever situate, lying, and being, or to be had, received, perceived or taken within the towns, hamlets, villages, fields and grounds of Stratford upon Avon, Old Stratford, Bishopton and Welcombe, or any of them, in the said county of Warwick. And also all that messuage or tenement with the appurtenances wherein one John Robinson dwelleth, situate, lying and being in the Blackfriars in London near the Wardrobe. And all other my lands, tenements, and hereditaments whatsoever.

To have and to hold all and singular the said premises with their appurtenances unto the said Susanna Hall during the term of her natural life. And after her decease to the first son of her body lawfully issuing and to the heirs males of the body of the said first son lawfully issuing. And for default of such issue to the second son of her body lawfully issuing, and to the heirs males of the said second son lawfully issuing. And for default of such heirs to the third son of the body of the said Susanna lawfully issuing and of the heirs males of the body of the said third son lawfully issuing. And for default of such issue the same so to be and remain to the fourth, fifth, sixth and seventh sons of her body lawfully issuing, one after another; and to the heirs males of the bodies of the said fourth, fifth, sixth and seventh sons lawfully issuing. In such manner as it is before limited to be and remain to the first, second and third sons of her body and to their heirs males.

And for default of such issue the said premises to be and remain to my said niece [grandchild] Hall and the heirs males of her body lawfully issuing. And for default of issue to my daughter Judith and the heirs males of her body lawfully issuing. And for default of such issue to the right heirs of me, the said William Shakespeare for ever.

Item, I give unto my wife my second best bed with the furniture. Item, I give and bequeath to my said daughter Judith my broad silver-gilt bowl.

All the rest of my goods, chattels, leases, plate, jewels and household stuff whatsoever, after my debts and legacies paid and my funeral expenses discharged, I give, devise and bequeath to my son-in-law John Hall, gentleman, and my daughter Susanna his wife, whom I ordain and make executors of this my last will and testament.

And I do entreat and appoint the said Thomas Russell, esquire, and Francis Collins, gentleman, to be overseers hereof. And do revoke all former wills and publish this to be my last will and testament. In witness whereof I have hereunto put my hand the day and year first above written.

By me William Shakespeare.

Witness to the
publishing hereof:
Francis Collins.
Julius Shaw
John Robinson.
Hamnet Sadler.
Robert Whattcot.

Inscription on his Tombstone:
Good friend, for Jesus' sake forbear
To dig the dust enclosèd here!
Blessed be the man that spares these stones,
And cursed be he that moves my bones.

[The Stratford friends singled out for bequests are, naturally enough, leading townsmen, the prosperous and well-to-do to whom the Shakespeare family belonged. Thomas Combe, to whom Shakespeare left his sword (itself a symbol of gentlemanly status), was the nephew and heir of the rich bachelor John Combe, who had lived in the house to which Holy Trinity's college of canons had been converted. John had left Shakespeare £5 in 1613 and has a fine effigy in the church from a Southwark workshop – who advised on that? – as was William's own. John increased his estate by money-lending, interest on which was restricted by statute to 10 per cent. Very early the following was attributed to William – no reason why it should not be his, nor the inscription on his grave either. Robert Greene said that he could turn his hand to anything, and he was a good hand at doggerel.

> Ten in the hundred the Devil allows,
> But Combe will have twelve, he swears and avows.
> If anyone asks who lies in this tomb,
> 'Oh', quoth the Devil, 'tis my John a Combe.'

Sir Thomas Russell of Strensham – on his death-bed Shakespeare forgot his knighthood – was at this time living at nearby Alderminster. Hamnet Sadler was an old family friend from early days, living at the corner of High Street and Sheep Street. Hamnet and Judith had been godparents of Shakespeare's boy Hamnet when baptised in church, on Candlemas day, 2 February 1585; he was buried there 11 August 1596. Hamnet and Hamlet are the same name, interchangeable with variants.

William Reynolds was a neighbour in Chapel Street, of a well-to-do Catholic family. Stratford was increasingly Protestant, even Puritan; but there was a notable Catholic minority, including one of the schoolmasters, Simon Hunt, who left to become a Jesuit, and succeeded Father Parsons as a Penitentiary at St Peter's, Rome.

Shakespeare's godson, young William Walker, baptised 16 October 1608 (a plague year, the year of *Pericles*, when Shakespeare is likely to have been away from London, at Stratford), was the son of Henry Walker, a prosperous mercer.

Anthony Nash, owner of the *Bear* inn, leading hostelry in the town, left it to his son Thomas, who married Shakespeare's granddaughter, Elizabeth, ten years later, in 1626. He died in 1647; two years later, something of an heiress, she married John Barnard, created a baronet at the Restoration. Lady Barnard had no children.

Of the witnesses, Julius Shaw lived next but one to New Place; Whatcott had given evidence for Susanna in 1613, when she brought an action for defamation against John Lane, junior, of Alveston.]